Recovering Our Children

Recovering Our Children

◆

A Handbook for Parents of Young People in Early Recovery

John C. Cates
and Jennifer Cummings

Writers Club Press
New York Lincoln Shanghai

Recovering Our Children
A Handbook for Parents of Young People in Early Recovery

Writers Club Press
an imprint of iUniverse, Inc.

For information address:
iUniverse, Inc.
2021 Pine Lake Road, Suite 100
Lincoln, NE 68512
www.iuniverse.com

Editor: Michael Sion

ISBN: 0-595-26428-X

Printed in the United States of America

Contents

Introduction

It was Saturday morning, about 10. A beautiful spring day, radiating health, warmth and safety. Jennifer, the co-author of this book, and I were sitting in a restaurant's party room. We were grabbing a few precious hours from each of our schedules to discuss some of the final needs in finishing this book. Jennifer excused herself for a moment, and I was left alone to ruminate on what I might write as an introduction.

As I sat, a group of 15 or so women entered, and began to celebrate in earnest their purpose for coming to the restaurant and asking for the party room. Each was clad in the most popular of suburbia's styles, their makeup perfect, and having a "good Texas hair day." Many were accompanied by one or two small children each. Two of these women were pregnant. Three of the number were in their 40s or 50s, while there also was one "grandma" of about 65 or 70 (also impeccably attired for the Houston suburb served by this particular establishment). The rest represented the best of their nation's army of young new mothers in their 20s.

THIS WAS A BABY SHOWER!

What a glorious occasion! The beginning of all of the hopes and dreams of parenthood. The coming of a young human to take his or her place in our great American society, and continue the line of achievement and virtue we hope all of our children pursue. I felt the surge of love coming from the young moms as they cared for their small children. I heard the pride in their voices as they recounted little Joey's latest exploits or accepted a compliment for little Mary's tiny Nike tennis shoes.

And then—this happy scene changed before my eyes . . .

These mothers now sat in my office in tears, terrified and hurt. The very toddlers and babies in front of me in the party room now were adolescents diagnosed with chemical dependency. The mothers and grandmothers stared at me in disbelief . . . it couldn't be . . . not Joey . . . not Mary! Now I could feel the all-too-familiar feelings of parents wrestling with emotions and the denial of the seriousness of the situation in which they now found their children and themselves.

Luckily for me that morning, Jennifer returned and saved me from my morose daydream; but I have not been able to shake the vision. No new parent dreams that she or he really will have to deal with a child contracting a catastrophic disease. This is especially true of an embarrassing catastrophic disease such as chemical addiction.

I mean, we as parents will be careful and protective . . . We will talk to our children and prepare them to stay away from those things that will make them sick . . . We will be involved and make sure our children stay involved in all the things that our culture has built to keep young minds occupied and out of trouble, activities such as sports, church, school and Scouts . . . and what does get by will in the end probably be a phase that they will grow out of naturally. I mean all children have some trouble, don't they? . . . I mean, we all had some wild-oat days and we grew out of them . . . didn't we?

THIS BOOK IS FOR the parents who find out that the disease of chemical dependency is Here and Now. This book is for the parent who got called to school because little Joey got caught with marijuana. This book is for the parents who heard little Mary on the phone with one of her friends talking about how "splashed" she got last Friday night as she continues to fail to perform in her college classes or on her new job. This book is for the parent who is beginning to hear the warning buzzers go off as he notices changes in his child's behavior, or hears of his child's friends starting to have trouble.

According to what the young people I know tell me, this book is for most of the parents of their fellow students. But most of all, this book is for parents who want their children to live, and are ready to begin the long but rewarding journey toward recovery.

This book contains the *beginning* of a plan for recovery. It is the *beginning* of a guide to help parents use one of the most powerful tools in helping to deal with their child's disease, the *alternative peer group*. Substance-abuse problems enter all parts of a sufferer's life. The addict uses and abuses school, friends, work, health, emotions, dreams—and especially families.

Because of the manipulative pervasiveness of the problems, recovery comes over a very long period of time and is characterized by twists and turns that make it impossible to effectively predict procedure more than a little bit at a time. Therefore, the successful parent will work hard at developing a *pattern of patience* in learning and implementing all that there is to learn about the disease.

It is my sincere hope that this book will especially help in the early days of successful recovery to unravel the rabbit trails and dark paths to nowhere that so plague parents at a time when they most need clear direction and explanations.

—John C. Cates

Foreword

Much of my professional effort has focused on finding effective and comprehensive treatments for adolescent substance abusers, addressing problems in the training of professionals, and examining the importance of parental involvement to the adolescent's sustained recovery. I have tested, treated, testified, rejoiced and grieved as I have worked in the area of adolescent substance abuse. This book is a godsend to families in distress.

If you are a treatment professional, I applaud you for reading this book. Having been trained as a psychologist myself, I will forewarn you that there may be perspectives taken in this book that will challenge traditional thinking about treatment. I have struggled against my own indoctrination as I have become more deeply involved in the support of families with addiction crises. I urge you to remain open to new possibilities. If you are a parent of a child with substance abuse problems, my heart and hope are with you.

Most of us are shocked when we discover, through our own crisis, the extent of the insanity in our culture. Cultures change slowly in almost imperceptible increments. I use the term 'imperceptible' because small changes are quite literally beyond the perceptual acuity of our sense organs. If you had left the planet some 50 years ago and were re-entering life in the United States today, the differences would be apparent and overwhelming. Seedling trees would appear to have become abruptly massive through changes that were assuredly taking place moment by moment out of our perceptual awareness. Similarly, you would see the blatant erosion of innocence that we just haven't noticed as we blithely go through life. We just didn't notice the insidious creeping of the age of onset of alcohol consumption from 17 to 16 to 15, etc. But now we have reached 12. More than half of the Caucasian adolescents surveyed by Warheit, Vega, Khoury, Gil, & Elfenbein (1996) had begun drinking alcohol by the age of 12. By the time the adolescents in the study had reached 14 years of age, almost three-fourths reported alcohol use, and almost one-third reported illicit drug use. The rates of use are similar but slightly lower for non-whites. Children are beginning to drink and engage in sexual activities at or before 12 and our culture has only now begun to awaken. In this era, drug abuse has become the norm rather than deviant. "In this society, drug use has become one aspect of this natural process to the extent that a teenager is deviant (from a normative perspective) if he or she has not tried alcohol, cigarettes, or marijuana by the completion of high school" (Newcomb & Bentler, 1989). A John Hopkins University study by Dr. Hoover Adger revealed a five-fold increase in the development of addiction if the child starts drinking before the age of 15.

We feel safer when we cling to the notion that substance abuse is the activity of the troubled, weird kids from broken or strange families. We assume that substance abuse is in response to some inner demons or personal problem. It's time to give that thinking up. When asked about their drug use, an alarming number of teenagers say that they first try drugs because that is what they think the cool or popular kids do. They keep using because it feels good. That's it. Some become addicted, mean, and miserable. Rarely can an addict see that their misery is associated with their drug use. It feels to them as if the misery comes from anyone or anything that gets in the way of their drug use. The adolescent's brain isn't fully developed, and therefore neither is his or her thinking. Add psychoactive substances to the equation and you have a very compromised ability to think clearly.

I once had a young student who read a research article that showed a correlation between hyperactivity in children and depression in mothers. She said, "If only someone would figure out how to effectively treat maternal depression, children wouldn't become hyperactive."

Adolescents think this way. Of course, this student's conclusion was inappropriate, just as is the traditional perspective that dysfunction in the family makes adolescents do drugs. It is at least as feasible to consider that the family is dysfunctional because the parents are living in fear for their child and too often for themselves, as well. The parent's actions in response to this fear (over-control of the adolescent, denial, withdrawal, etc.) are almost always driven by their love for their child. The result, unfortunately, is that their denial feels like neglect to the child. Their over-control feels like cruelty. Ultimately, it creates another excuse for the teenager to act out. Of course, the parents then tend to do more of the same, hoping to get through to the child. The cycle finally stymies all and the family is paralyzed. The situation hasn't gotten better, the action isn't working, and parents run out of ideas. It is time to try something new.

The nation's largest and most expensive drug prevention program, DARE, has failed and has, in fact, been repeatedly proved to increase, not decrease, future drug use by children who participate in the program (Donaldson, Graham, Piccinin, & Hansen, 1995). The first admitted heroin user I met was the essay winner for the DARE program in Chicago some 10 years or so ago. Why? One can only speculate. Teenagers are conformists. They think that most of the other kids are getting high. They usually overestimate the frequencies of use by their peers. Most professionals recognize that DARE was not designed to deal with this normal developmental fact of adolescence. The program fails to recognize that children's commitment is meaningless without ongoing support, particularly if they think it will make them an outcast. Our government is finally ending the flow of funds into a program that actually harms our children.

So what can a parent do? Too often parents report that they had spent years trying (often secretly) various treatments for their child when he or she began to exhibit signs of disturbance.

Adolescents are averaging 36 months of failed treatment apiece before "getting caught" and entering rehabilitation treatment for substance abuse. This three years usually is spent in an average of four or more separate treatments prior to entering treatment for chemical dependency (Edens, 2001).

As the incidence of adolescent substance abuse has risen dramatically, the treatment community has struggled to develop treatments that are tailored to the issues and perspectives of the adolescent. Most parents look to their pediatrician, a psychiatrist or a psychologist when they decide to seek help with their child's behavior problems. Initial treatments usually involve individual therapy, and they typically fail. Rarely are these initial treatments focused on alcohol or drug use. In fact, 75 percent of initial prior providers either are unaware that the adolescent is using drugs or alcohol or choose not to divulge this information to the parent.

Many adolescents in substance-abuse treatment programs report having been treated for psychiatric disorders other than substance abuse prior to being "caught" with illegal substances. These adolescents report giving false information to their treatment professionals in order to hide their substance abuse and, in fact, to keep a supply of prescription medications flowing. About 60% of adolescent substance abusers in individual therapy are being prescribed medication for a psychiatric disorder. After treatment, ongoing pharmacological treatments tend to be required for only 20 percent of the substance abusers. Psychiatric diagnoses of adolescent substance abusers usually include major depression, attention deficit disorder, oppositional defiant disorder, adjustment disorder, bipolar disorder, anxiety disorder, personality disorder N.O.S, and Tourette's Syndrome. Consequently they are provided with psychiatric medications, which they abuse or sell. Psychiatric symptoms in most of the adolescents tend to remit upon sustained sobriety.

One young addict in treatment, whom I interviewed was taking seven prescribed medications simultaneously before entering treatment for substance abuse. She is from a large, warm, highly educated, intact family, who were trying desperately to help her by providing the best medical care they could for their highly disturbed daughter. It was very difficult for them to accept the possibility that she was merely an addict. After she ran away from home and spent six weeks prostituting and stealing for drugs, the police found her and she was taken to the county psychiatric hospital where she remained until her detoxification was complete. None of her prescriptions was renewed. Her subsequent work in treatment was long and hard, exhausting both herself and her parents, but she is now chemical free and going to college on an academic scholarship.

Use of psychoactive substances (alcohol, LSD, marijuana, cocaine, ecstasy, etc.) can result in the development of psychological symptoms such as anxiety, combativeness, paranoia, toxic psychosis, sexual acting out and depression (Facts, http). According to a policy set forth by the American Academy of Child and Adolescent Psychiatry in 1990, drug and alcohol screening is strongly encouraged whenever an adolescent is presented for treatment. AACAP guidelines urge psychiatrists to systematically consider substance abuse as a possibility to rule out in adolescent patients, since substance abuse creates symptoms that appear as a psychiatric disorder (Policy, 1997, hap). However, a recent report on the abilities of physicians to detect and diagnose substance abuse problems indicated that 41 percent of pediatricians and 94 percent of primary care physicians "fail to diagnose drug abuse when presented with a classic description of an adolescent patient with symptoms of drug abuse" (Califano, 2000, p. i). Substance abuse is the largest category of mental disorders in the United States in terms of the number of people effected, and yet 90 percent of the doctoral training programs in psychology have no requirement of any course that specifically addresses substance abuse issues (Edens, 2001).

The training of professionals is not the only problem. Substance abusers are better and better able to hide their use. They know the lists of suspicious behaviors that are handed out at PTA meetings by well-intended counselors. If you ask them directly, they lie. How many adolescents, whether they are in trouble or not, are going to sit down face to face and bare their innermost secrets to an adult? This may be even less likely when Mom and Dad are paying that adult. One young man who had wasted $46,800 seeing a psychiatrist twice weekly for three years told me after he had been sober for several years, "it was easier to get away with lying to one adult for three years than it was lying to 50 of my peers for one day." Mental health professionals repeatedly assume first of all that their adolescent patients tell them the truth and second that any drug use that may be suspected is a secondary problem, not the primary issue. This is just wrong. You cannot effectively interact and facilitate change in a person who is high on drugs. One young man in recovery gloated over his ability to have tricked his therapist by being high on multiple substances during most of his sessions.

The realities that reduce the adolescent's ability to deal effectively with drug and alcohol use within traditional treatment programs or without intervention are:

1. Adolescents assume that adults don't know what they are talking about when it comes to drugs, alcohol, and sex (and they might be right).

 2. Peers are the primary role models and sources of information, influence and esteem.

 3. Having fun is a basic need that holds priority over most other needs.

 4. It is OK and usually necessary to lie to adults to protect our peers, our culture, and ourselves.

 5. Parents are focused on the wrong things (achievement, clean rooms, nice haircuts, etc.).

The Alternative Peer Group (APG) model for treatment developed out of a grass-roots effort to devise a treatment milieu that works with the realities of the adolescent culture. The APG treatment model follows a basic 12-step format as the primary vessel, but the program is structured around a system of parent and adolescent meetings, group therapies, and leisure, leadership and educational activities. Adolescents are likely to need 18 to 36 months of treatment. During this time, they learn to stay away from adolescents who are not in recovery, learn how to interact appropriately with both peers and adults, and learn how to have fun without chemicals. Parents are asked to make the same commitment in terms of time and self-exploration. This is not always because the parents need so much treatment for parenting. Addicts just need something different from their parents, and the parents need all the help and support they can get.

Is parental commitment really necessary to the adolescent's recovery? Some parents are so frustrated and tired by the time they reach us that they say, "It's his problem, not mine. Why should I have to come?" Parents of alcoholic or drug-addicted kids are usually tired, angry, scared, and depressed unless they have been capable of avoiding the reality of their child's addiction. Most parents don't really like the idea of participating in their child's program when it keeps them from doing many of their social activities, keeps them up late, asks that they learn some things about recovery, and encourages self-exploration. But kids whose parents don't get involved generally drop out of treatment. Sometimes kids drop out anyway, but if the parents stay involved, their children are more likely to return to treatment. Adolescents in treatment whose parents participate consistently are more likely to achieve sustained sobriety than are those whose parents do not participate. Those who drop out are often injured or killed in alcohol or drug-related automobile accidents, are more likely to suicide, are more likely to overdose or participate in criminal activities for which they may be arrested, and/or at the very least will have to be placed back into treatment at a later date. The longer it takes for a child to get the right treatment, the more pronounced his or her emotional, cognitive, and social immaturity will be.

Some adolescents receive their first substance abuse treatment when they overdose and are taken to a hospital for detoxification and the standard 30-day inpatient treatment. The most common recommendation when a child is released from hospitalization is that he or she attend 12-step meetings. However, youth motivation to attend is rarely intrinsic, and may be stymied by the primarily adult composition of most group meetings (Kelly, Myers, & Brown, 2000). In fact, Kelly and Myers (1997) found that adolescents who attend groups largely comprised of other teens fared substantially better on outcome measures than did adolescents attending adult meetings. Joseph Nowinski has found that adolescents are best treated in a group that he terms the "therapeutic tribe" (Nowinski, 1990). APG treatment offers a unique opportunity for adolescents to recover from alcohol and/or drug abuse or dependence within the parameters of normal adolescent development.

The authors of this book are leaders in the APG treatment arena and know well the despair that haunts our homes when our children are out of control. Within these pages you will find a hand to hold and a gentle voice that can guide you through the heartache to a happy outcome.

Anette Edens, Ph.D.
Assistant Professor
Psychology Department
University of St. Thomas
Houston, Texas

Bentler, P. M. (1995). EQS Structural Equations Program Manual. Encino, CA:Multivariate Software, Inc.

Califano, J. A. (1999) Back to school 1999—National Survey of American Attitudes on substance abuse V: Teens and their parents, Introductory remarks. The National Center on Addiction and Substance Abuse. Columbia University.

Chassin, L., Pitts, S. C., & Prost, J. (2002) Binge drinking trajectories from adolescence to emerging adulthood in a high-risk sample: Predictors of substance abuse outcomes. Journal of Consulting and Clinical Psychology, 70(1), 67–78.

Chiert, T., Gold, A. N., & Taylor, J. (1994). Substance abuse training in APA-accredited doctoral programs in clinical psychology: A survey. Professional Psychology: Research and Practice, 25(1), 8084.

Donaldson, S. L., Graham, J. W., Piccinin, A. M. & Hansen, W. B. (1995). Resistance-skills training and onset of alcohol use: Evidence for beneficial and potentially harmful effects in public schools and in private Catholic schools. Health Psychology, 14(4), 291–300.

Edens, A., Barajas, O., Khawaja, I., & Wilson, D. (2001a). Treatment histories of adolescents entering substance abuse treatment. Paper presented at the 47th annual meeting of the Southwestern Psychological Association, Houston, Texas, April 12–14, 2001.

Edens, A., Wilson, D., Quintanilla, M., & Kiev, J. (2001b). Drug and alcohol diagnosis and treatment training in doctoral programs. Paper presented at the 47th annual meeting of the Southwestern Psychological Association, Houston, Texas, April 12–14, 2001.

Epstein, H. T. (1980). EEG developmental stages. Developmental Psychology, 13, 629–531.

Facts about cocaine. [Online]. The Houston Council on Alcohol & Drug Abuse. http://www.council-houston.org/cocaine.htm> [1998, March 3].

Gonet, M. M. (1994). Counseling the adolescent substance abuser. Thousand Oaks, CA:Sage.

Kelly, J. F. & Myers, M. G. (1997). Adolescent treatment outcome in relation to adolescent 12-step group attendance. Alcoholism: Clinical and Experimental Research, 21,27A.

Kelly, J. F., Myers, M. G., & Brown, S. A. (2000). A multivariate process model of adolescent 12-step attendance and substance use outcome following inpatient treatment. Psychology of Addictive Behaviors, 14(4), 376–389.

Lubin, B., Brady, K., Woodward, L., & Thomas, E. A. (1986). Graduate professional psychology training in alcoholism and substance abuse: 1984, Professional Psychology: Research and Practice, 12, 151–154.

Miller, W. R., & Brown, S. A. (1997). Why psychologists should treat alcohol and drug problems. American Psychologist, 52(12), 1269–1279.

Nelson, C. B., Heath, A. H., & Kessler, R. C. (1998). Temporal progression of alcohol dependence symptoms in the U. S. household population: Results from the National Comorbidity Study, Journal of Consulting and Clinical Psychology, 66(3), 474–483.

Newcomb, M. D., & Bentler, P. M. (1989) Substance use and abuse among children and teenagers. American Psychologist, 44(2), 242–248.

Nowinski, J. (1999). Self-help groups for addictions. In B. S. McCrady & E. E. Epstein (Eds.), Addictions: A comprehensive guidebook. (pp. 328–346). New York, NY: Oxford University Press.

Policy statement: Drug and alcohol screening.(1997). Online]. American Academy of Child and Adolescent Psychiatry. <http://www.aacap.org/publications/policy/ps12.htm> [1998, September 7].

Santrock, J. W. (1998). Adolescence, (7th edition). Boston, MA:McGraw Hill.

Schlesinger, S. E., & Barg, D. (1987). Substance misuse training for psychiatry residents. Journal of Psychiatric Education, 11(2), 87–99.

Selin, J. A., & Svanum, S. (1981). Alcoholism and substance training: A survey of graduate programs in clinical psychology. Professional Psychology: Research and Practice, 12, 717–721.

Warheit, G. J., Vega, W. A., Khoury, E. L., Gil, A. A., & Elfenbein, P. H. (1996). A comparative analysis of cigarette, alcohol, and illicit drug use among an ethnically diverse sample of Hispanic, African American, and non-Hispanic White adolescents, Journal of Drug Issues, 26(4), 901–922.

Wills, T. A., Sandy, J. M., Yaeger, A., & Shinar, O. (2001). Family risk factors and adolescent substance use: Moderation effects for temperament dimensions. Developmental Psychology, 37(3) 283–297.

PART I
The Path

1

Your Young Person Is Sick

It is *not* your fault.

None of us are perfect parents. Some of us are very poor parents. Yet there are children who grow up in abusive homes who never use drugs or alcohol. And there are children from non-abusive "good homes" who do.

Parenting plays one of the greatest roles in shaping our children's behavior, but we do not get to raise our children in a controlled environment, nor are we the only big influence on their lives. There are other worlds within their worlds—both real and illusory. There is the world of their peers, at school and in the neighborhood. There is the world of sex, drugs and violence they are bombarded with by television and movies, videos and music.

We cannot shelter our children from every negative influence, nor can we provide an impenetrable shield against substance abuse. But we *can* be one of the greatest factors contributing to the recovery of a young person using drugs or alcohol. When parents are willing to get involved in the recovery process, the young person's chances of recovery are very high. When parents do *not* get involved, some kids will still recover, but the chances of early recovery are greatly diminished. These young people generally suffer longer, and with far more serious consequences, before they get sober. And those who aren't as fortunate, of course, don't survive the disease.

To be the most effective in a child's recovery program, parents must become educated about the disease and be open to learning the tools of recovery.

Begin now to understand that chemical addiction is a disease—a real disease, as real as leukemia or diabetes. It has neurochemical components and psychological components. In many cases, there is a great probability of a genetic component. Chemical addiction is progressive, chronic and—if not put into remission—terminal. Having this disease is much like having leukemia or a brain tumor. It is that deadly, and must be put into remission as soon as possible.

The disease of addiction is cunning, baffling and powerful. It affects the thinking process, such that an addict's mind tricks him into further drug use through rationalization and justification. Have you ever been on a diet and had your brain convince you that it makes perfect sense to eat a piece of cake, then afterward you wonder how you could have thought that it was the right thing to do? That kind of trickery is immeasurably worse when the brain is experiencing the euphoric highs and anxiety-ridden lows that spring from chemical use, abuse and addiction.

The good news is that experts know how to put this disease into remission. As a parent, you must be open to learning new tools and techniques for parenting a young person affected by substance abuse. The quicker and better you learn these skills, the more effective you will be.

So get ready.

If you do nothing more than show up at the parent meetings each week, you will get to hear from other parents in the group what works and what does not. These meetings are a very important source of information. If you want to learn as quickly as possible, we recommend that at the beginning you attend at least two meetings a week. Think of these meetings as parenting classes. Attend any other special classes offered to parents in the program. And read this book.

Remain open to learning new things. New actions are necessary to bring about new results. These new parenting tools will seem different, and some will be difficult to practice, but they are simple tools that will make life easier for everyone in your family. They will make the difference between beating your head against a wall and drawing a line where needed. They will be steps that you have the power to take—and you will not be alone. Others will be available to help.

Choose to have faith. No matter what your son's or daughter's history may be, there is a very high probability that they'll make it in recovery because they have at least one parent who loves them and is willing to learn. Everything is possible from this point, from where your family stands today. And now is the perfect time to begin.

First Suggestions for Parents:

- Go to parent meetings

- Get to know the other parents in the group; use the phone list

- Create a chemical-free home

- Set a few principles for living that are required for living in your home (include working a program of recovery)

- Let go of things that are not the highest priority right now (sobriety is; grades aren't)

- Start learning everything you can about the disease and recovery

As parents, we can't force our children to recover and grow. Even God will not do that. But we can light the way. And just as the moon reflects the rays from the sun, we can reflect God's love as our sons and daughters work their way out of the darkness of their disease.

2

Getting Started

Many parents who come into the program have already done everything they could think of to save their child. Even parents in denial of their young person's substance abuse have done what they could to control the child's behavior. Many parents have enlisted the help of various mental-health professionals, heard a variety of possible diagnoses and tried "promising" medications. They may have spent fortunes on treatment centers and survival camps. Often, parents turn to a recovery program after everything else has failed. Parents enter the program feeling helpless, hopeless, exhausted, powerless, desperate and even betrayed.

This chapter discusses a few new approaches for parents to use that will be empowering to them as well as the recovering addict. By trying a few new moves, parents can begin to regain their strength and sanity.

It Is Not *Your Fault*

Please know that we know that it is *not* your fault that your son or daughter has this disease. Unless you put alcohol in the baby bottle or cocaine in the sugar bowl, it is not your fault, no matter what else you did or did not do in raising your child. If you are like all the other parents who have come into the program and have been doing what you could for your child to the best of your knowledge and ability—no matter if you believe you made one million mistakes—*IT IS NOT YOUR FAULT.*

Let Your Young Person Own His or Her Behavior

One of the most powerful things you can do to help your child get sober is to let the child own the decisions he has made. The *child* chose to use. With all of the bad and good circumstances the child had going in life, *he* chose to use. There always will be a host of circumstances that substance abusers can cite to rationalize and justify their abuse. But it is in the face of any and all circumstances that *the child* will have to choose to be sober. The child can do this only by owning his or her behavior. You empower your son or daughter in sobriety by letting go of blaming yourself and letting the young person take responsibility for his or her actions. You are responsible *to* your children, not *for* them.

> **You empower your son or daughter in recovery by letting go of blaming yourself and letting your young person take responsibility for his or her actions.**

Become Aware of Your Enabling Behaviors

Parents of substance abusers generally are enablers. Enablers are people who make it possible for someone to continue to use drugs or alcohol, by inadvertently providing the financing, or by protecting users from the consequences of their actions. Adult addicts are more quickly faced with the consequences of their drug use than are young people. If adults are unable to perform at their job, they get fired. If they don't have a job, they don't get paid. If they don't have an income, they don't have a place to live or money to buy food. If an adult addict doesn't have someone to take care of him, the addict feels the consequences fairly quickly.

Young people living with their parents have quite a different experience. They may be flunking out of school—or not going to school—but they have a nice home to live in, meals provided (and probably prepared) for them, clothes, spending money and "maid" service. Many have cars to drive with their parents paying for the car, insurance, maintenance and gas. Some parents even pay their children's traffic tickets.

 This all contributes to the cultural phenomenon we call *suburbanitus affluenza*. So many goodies—so little responsibility. Parents create this environment because they want to be good to their kids. But such coddling has negative effects. Having without earning actually feeds an unhealthy ego and weakens self-esteem. To get and stay sober, young people need to develop a healthy self-esteem/ego balance.

By supplying money and by protecting them from the consequences of their actions, parents enable their kids to continue using drugs. Parents need to become aware of their enabling behaviors. Supplying cash is usually one such behavior. Let your sons and daughters start earning their spending money. This will build their self-esteem.

> **Having without earning feeds an unhealthy ego and weakens self-esteem.**

Pick Your Battles

Families of users are usually embroiled in negative issues about the children's messy rooms, clothes, friends, smoking, bad language, grades, chores and lack of responsibility. Most interactions between parents and substance-abusing kids revolve around these issues. As a result, kids spend as little time at home as possible to avoid as much of the friction as they can.

It is important for all young people to be accountable and to begin to take responsibility. But they cannot succeed at being responsible about everything all at once. Parents need to pick the issues they want to address and keep matters simple.

We recommend that parents choose two to five principles that must be adhered to by anyone living in their home. What these principles are depend upon the family and the problems the young person is facing.

Change from this:

> *"Clean your room before you go out." "Sit up straight." "I don't like your friends." "You have to do the dishes three times a week. If you only do them twice you have to come home one hour early on Sunday. If you only do them once . . ." "Change into something decent." "We aren't paying private school tuition so that you can get C's and D's." "If I catch you smoking one more time, you're grounded." "How much homework do you have tonight?" "Don't roll your eyes at me!"*

To something like this:

Requirements for Living in Our Home

- No use of mind-changing chemicals

- Stick with winners

- Work of recovery to our satisfaction

- Obey the laws

- Tell the truth

This list will be different for different families. One family may need to include: *No physical or verbal abuse.* Another might include: *Attend school.*

Later, after the young person has achieved some sobriety and learned some of the tools of recovery, he will enter into what we call second-stage recovery. At that time the young person needs to be responsible for more than getting and staying sober. He needs to be responsible for full-time school or full-time work, or part-time of each. If the young person does not learn to be responsible in this way, he won't be able to stay sober. At the outset, however, learning to get and stay sober is enough.

Once you have established the key principles for living in your home, consider the rest secondary and, for now, try to let it go. It is not that the responsibility of work and school are not important. They are. But only if your child is alive. Your young person cannot give you everything right away. But if everyone stays focused on a few things, success is possible.

Also, getting *you* to let go of issues such as smoking and hair styles for awhile is one of the tools that makes the recovery program attractive to the kids.

> **Let go of secondary issues that are not immediate threats to your young person's life.**

If this is hard for you, remember that you are fighting a deadly disease. If your child had leukemia, would you insist that your child submit to chemotherapy if that's what the doctor recommended? Of course you would. But would you make your child clean his room before he went to the hospital? Of course not.

When you let go of these secondary issues—*really* let them go. Don't do your child's job and your job both. If your child needs to focus on recovery and hanging out with the group, you can let go of grades. Your young person doesn't have to let go of grades. But it's better if <u>*you* do</u>. Take a break from this anxiety. You no longer have to do your son's algebra. And don't even consider doing his history project. Parents who have been over-involved in their child's schoolwork find this a great relief.

Does your daughter smoke? If she is in early recovery, we suggest you let this go for now. Smoking could kill her, but it doesn't put her in immediate danger the way that drugs do. Kids using drugs can kill themselves tonight with an overdose, or get shot in the course of a drug deal, or die in a fatal car crash. Your daughter probably cannot handle quitting smoking while dealing with early recovery. Let her get sober; later she will probably decide to quit smoking on her own. If she doesn't get sober, she will probably not be able to think clearly about the dangers of smoking.

The behaviors you require from your child should be determined by the level of the disease you are fighting. Some young people coming into the program can, at the beginning, handle some rules from second-stage recovery. The determination of the early rules appropriate to your situation should be set with the help of a counselor.

> **Some young people can accept rules for second-stage recovery at the beginning. Seek the help of the counselor to determine rules appropriate to your case.**

Create a Home Environment that Supports Recovery

Do not have liquor in your home. Do not let other people use drugs or alcohol in your home. If you drink, we recommend that you consider what the effects may be on your child while he is in the early stages of recovery.

Do not keep liquor in your home.

If you are a social drinker, this may be inconvenient and seem unnecessary to you at first. But it is very important to your young person's chances of success. Consider what you would do if you had a child with diabetes. Would you keep a lot of cakes around the house? Would you serve brownies to the adults after dinner? No, you would serve treats that everyone could safely enjoy.

Parents can learn the behaviors that young people must learn to get and stay sober, and model these behaviors for their kids. It may feel like your kids aren't watching you or, when they do, are rejecting everything they see. But it isn't true. Unconsciously they are absorbing what you do as a model for what they are eventually going to grow into. And it is what you do, not what you say, that has this impact.

Your actions speak louder than your words.

Many parents try very hard to find the right words to say to their young person to give them the perfect message that will make the difference. The perfect message does not come in words; the perfect message is your demonstration of what you wish to teach.

The next chapter discusses what young people need to do and to learn to get sober, and parents can do to support them. Below are statements from a few of the kids in the program attesting to the importance of parents in the children's recovery. Note the importance they place on their parents' taking a stand and working their own programs.

Carol, 18 (13 when she first came into the program):

I wouldn't be sober if it weren't for my parents and if they weren't sober. When I first got sober I hadn't used a lot of drugs yet and I worked a pretty superficial program. When I relapsed I started using a lot. Looking back, I surprised myself. I didn't know I really was an addict. My mother asked me to start working a program again and told me that I would have to work a program or I couldn't live with her any more. I said fine and left with my friends. When I came back, the doors were locked and the locks were changed. I stayed with my friends and continued using. After three days of being awake and using cocaine and heroin, I went to my mom's work and asked her to put me in the hospital. I'm still in early recovery and it's still hard, but I know my mom has these clear boundaries. I know that if I go back to using, I can lose my family. Now I know I have a safe place, my mother understands what I'm going through and is supportive—I can talk to her about everything. I don't think I would be sober if my parents were using or if they weren't holding me accountable.

Bob, 18 (15 when he entered the program):

My parents being in the program is very beneficial to me now. And I can see how kids whose parents aren't in the program don't progress and are in the program forever. Every kid, whether they admit to it or not, wants to live up to their parents' expectations. Sometimes I don't want to go to the meeting and I think about my parents being in the program and doing what they should be doing and it makes me want to do what I should be doing. I couldn't fix their issues for them. If I was dealing with my issues and they weren't working a program and weren't making progress on their issues, it wouldn't be working. We're all changing together—they are not giving in to the old ways. It's good to be able to talk to them, too. And being in the program together has given us a lot to talk about.

Denny, 17 (15 when he entered the program):

Before and while I was using, I was ungrateful. As soon as my mother kicked me out, it was a lesson in gratitude. When I was out of the house and sleeping on the streets or in rehab I really missed her and I knew how much I loved her. I've kept that in mind ever since. [Did your mother kick you out or did she give you some options?] *I kept screwing up. She found a place for me to stay and I kept screwing up there. The more she didn't let me get up on my own, the more I screwed up. She gave me a list of boundaries and I didn't care, and I knew I was choosing to have to leave. The last time, she didn't find me a place to stay. I fell and she let me fall and she let me get up by myself. But she was still there for me. She was there talking to me and I felt her support. And that meant a lot to me.*

Jennifer, 18 (14 when she entered the program):

I wouldn't have gotten sober if my parents didn't make me start going to meetings. They didn't give me a choice. My dad would drag me to the car and I would be crying. At first I didn't think I belonged in the group. I thought I was better than everybody else. After I got to know people, I felt like I belonged. I hadn't used hard drugs. I drank a lot on the weekends, and during the week I took a lot of caffeine pills and diet pills. I did it basically because I didn't like myself, who I was. I was depressed a lot of the time. And I did it for acceptance. I didn't care about my life. I know that if my parents hadn't made me get sober, I would have used more and gotten worse.

3

Recovering in an Integrated, Alternative Peer-Group Program

"There's nothing wrong with teenagers that reasoning with them won't aggravate."

—Anonymous

There are two things addicts must do to get and stay off mind-changing chemicals. They must establish and develop their relationship with a power greater than themselves. And they must change their friends. Many times, the second must be accomplished before starting the first. The purpose of an integrated, spiritual-based, alternative peer-group program is to promote both actions.

Addicts cannot stay sober if they spend time with friends who use. This was recognized by Alcoholics Anonymous decades ago when the organization coined the phrase, "Stick with winners."

Carefully chosen winners help each other grow. In the recovery program, winners will be able to learn and teach the tools of recovery, model them and hold each other accountable.

The idea of sticking with winners offends some people at first. It can seem as if we are turning our backs on friends who need our help. But the truth is that until you are sober and strong in recovery, you cannot help other addicts. They can pull you down, but you can't help them up. It's like the safety instructions on an airplane: First put on your own oxygen mask, then help the child next to you put on his.

Selecting the right peer groups in the pursuit of living a meaningful, constructive and fulfilling life always has been important. This has been recognized for thousands of years. A quick review of classical literature reveals powerful and influential writers indicating that it is a mark of wisdom for a human being to take great care in the selection and cultivation of a peer group. King Solomon said this 3,000 years ago: "He who walks with the wise grows wise, but a companion of fools suffers harm." (*Proverbs: 13:20.*)

"Stick with winners" is good advice for everyone. But it is critical counsel for those in recovery, and especially young people, who are so influenced by their peers.

Sticking with winners is essential for a young person in early recovery.

As important as it is, it is very hard to get people suffering from the disease of addiction to embrace the idea of changing their friends when they come into the program. Teenagers' friendships are their connection to the social world of their peers. For a teenager to drop her friendships is to drop her identity and connections to her world—to become no one nowhere.

Teenagers will not drop their old friends unless they have at least one new friend in place. A key intention of an alternative peer-group program is to accelerate the establishment of new friendships. A good program will provide a supply of "winners," teach the importance of sticking with winners and how to choose them. And the group feedback will hold teenagers accountable for their choices.

Who are 'Winners'?

So who is a winner for your child? You may be surprised. There is a whole continuum of winners and losers for kids in recovery.

We can begin with the children with whom your child has been getting loaded and who still are using. It is easy to eliminate these kids as possible winners. For your child, they are losers. The term "losers" may sound cruel. We do not mean by it that those kids are permanent losers in life. They are kids who may turn their lives around and make a tremendous contribution to the world. However, right now they are losers for your child because they will not hold him accountable or encourage his personal growth. They will provide an invitation to relapse.

The next group of losers is not as obvious to parents. These are kids whom you believe are sober, but are not verifiably so. These could be the neighborhood kids who were on the same Little League or softball team as your child two years ago. Or they could be kids from your church's youth group—kids whose parents you have known 15 years and whose kids you are sure are clean. These kids can be divided into two groups: those who actually use and those who do not. But you don't know which kids are in which group.

There are a number of kids who seem to be able to control their use or can abstain from using with no outside help. These kids are dangerous company for a dependent kid. Observing "controlled use" is an enticement to use. "It's OK for her, it's OK for me. She can do it, so I can do it, too." Yet the dependent user *can't* do it. And the kids who are able to abstain from using without help from outside of themselves also will challenge your child to do it on her own rather than learn the tools of recovery that include support of a recovery group. Also, not having learned the tools of recovery, they cannot teach them.

Kids who are verifiably sober, but have never used and, therefore, are not in recovery may seem like they would be a good influence on a young person in recovery, but actually may not be. First, I'm not sure how these kids would be verified as sober, but let's assume that here. A limited exposure to these kids, combined with a lion's share of exposure to winners (whom we will define in the next paragraph), will probably not damage your child. For some kids who have barely used, a large exposure to this group of kids may be good, and even sufficient as a group of winners with whom to associate. Whether your child is one of the kids for whom this is true can be determined by the program counselor, but only after several months of assessment.

Kids who have used and have embraced recovery have a lot to offer. These are the winners with whom you desire your child to bond. These kids can reach out to the kids coming into the program, relate to them, teach them that it's cool to get sober, and show them how to do it.

For a young person who is new in the program, real winners are those who have embraced sobriety and learned some of the tools of recovery. Ideally, they will be verifiably sober and participating in the same recovery program.

For a young person entering the program, a winner is someone who has embraced sobriety and is learning the tools of recovery.

Most parents initially assume that the kids who have never used are better qualified as winners than the kids who have used and are working on recovery. In fact, when parents first see these kids in the program, they often think they do not even want their child exposed to them.

This is understandable. Young people in early recovery look pretty much like they did before they came into the program. Some look bizarre. Some look like drug addicts. Some look like criminals. Some look like rebellious teenagers. Yet some, too, look like (and are) Boy Scouts and Girl Scouts. The number of "straight-looking" kids coming into the program has been increasing rapidly in recent years.

Once parents get to know these other kids in recovery, these children begin to appear more respectable. To some extent, after the kids have some sobriety, they start dressing and decorating themselves in ways that are more palatable to parents. But the real difference is the look of health, self-esteem and spiritual connection that parents see in the eyes and faces of these kids. They usually have not changed much with regard to their dress, but the parents discover that these kids can no longer be judged by that criterion. Over time, parents see that these kids are dedicated to living principle-based lives, working on their conscious contact with their higher power through prayer and meditation. They are using the tools of recovery and reaching out to newcomers in the group. They are practicing the unconditional love and acceptance that your child receives when he starts coming to meetings.

You may worry about your child being exposed to kids who have taken harder drugs or committed worse offenses than your child has. It is likely that there will be such kids in the program—unless your child has "done it all." But it also is true that your child has already been exposed to far more dangers than you are aware. And what your child has not done, he probably has friends who have. The young people who come into recovery are not innocents who need to be protected from reality. They have seen a lot and need to learn how to live in reality. And what of the young people in the program who have done more and worse? They will give your child the benefit of their experience, and can be a demonstration of what God can do for people who choose to get well. One of these "worst" cases could very well turn out to be the most important positive influence in your child's recovery.

> **The worst-looking kid in the program could turn out to be the most important positive influence in your child's recovery.**

As for kids who never used, they probably do not have a lot to offer at this time. For one thing, your son or daughter probably will not relate to them. Also, they cannot teach your young person how to get sober.

The young people in the program can.

Integrated Alternative Peer Group Programs And How They Support The Two Required Behaviors Of Recovery

An integrated, alternative peer-group program is not just a bunch of kids in recovery who are going to meetings and hanging out together. The program is more structured and is staffed by trained counselors. It can incorporate individual and/or group therapy. It also provides accountability.

Certain members of the group are chosen to help lead the group by serving on committees—usually a Reach Out Committee and a Steering Committee. Reach Out does just that. These kids reach out to newcomers and provide an orientation to the program for those attending their first meeting. The Steering Committee leads the regular meetings and, with the counselor, plans the other activities of the group.

Meetings

The program provides scheduled recovery meetings (usually two each week) and a constant flow of social activities. Some of the activities are planned and monitored by the staff, but more commonly they are activities that would be typical of any group of young people and parents—just without the alcohol (or drugs), and with a strong emphasis on emotional responsibility. Also, when needed, the kids can participate in either one-on-one counseling or group counseling.

The meetings are similar to Alcoholics Anonymous meetings except that they are generally more fun (more screaming and more laughing). During the meetings, the kids take turns sharing their experiences, strength and hope. By sharing their experiences and how the tools of recovery are working for them, the kids teach each other how to get sober. They also get to know each other's feelings and thoughts.

Social Activities

After meetings the group meets for "coffee." It would be more accurate to say that the kids meet informally at a nearby restaurant or someone's house. The time is used for one-on-one sharing and simply spending time together for fun. Friendships develop. The kids get to know each other quickly, and they build relationships that become powerful and influential.

A Program of Attraction

An alternative, peer-group program is a program of attraction. It attracts newcomers with fun activities, counselors and the presence of other recovering young people to whom they can relate. It delivers the hope of getting their lives back. Making the program attractive to kids is critical. If the program stopped being fun—if we replaced the functions with study halls and tutoring opportunities—the kids would stop coming and the program would cease to exist.

Teaching through Socialization

Fun is essential. But these *functions* provide far more than that. All of the group activities provide opportunities to learn the principles and tools of recovery. The young people in the group are practicing these tools, teaching these principles to each other, demonstrating them, talking about them and honoring them. The "outlaw" mindset is replaced with a healthy mindset where what is "cool" includes sharing your feelings, getting honest, behaving responsibly with self-esteem, making amends, reaching out to newcomers, working a program, developing a relationship with a higher power and demonstrating unconditional love.

The group creates a community in which principle-based living and having a relationship with God is cool. This alternative community provides the fertile ground for young addicts to get rooted in recovery. These young people have been living in an insane world with insane ideals. In the group, they are able to embrace sane principles for living with friends who are doing the same. And where there was chaos, confusion and fear, the kids begin to experience some clarity and inner peace.

Accountability of Staff

There are other ways that the alternative peer group aids the recovery process. For one, this group of kids can provide counselors with what they have no other means to attain—real accountability. The kids themselves are the only ones who can really tell us whether a young person is following their treatment protocol—that is, working their program. Without this information, the kids are able to scam for a long, long time the very people who are trying to help them. The kids in the group do not see the counselor as the enemy the way that most young users view adults. Instead, the kids see substance abuse as the enemy—and a deadly one. And they see it as their duty to their friends to let the counselor know if one of the group is not doing what is needed to get or stay sober. With this information, the counselor is able to intervene quickly and effectively, when needed.

Accountability to Parents

Peer-group feedback also helps parents. Through the young people's group, parents receive reliable information about what their child actually is doing. Parents tend to be very fearful of accusing their young person of anything if they are not very sure that it is true. Once the parents get to know and trust some of the other kids, they also trust the information that comes from the kids.

Accountability of Parents

The parent group also provides accountability for often-skewed family dynamics. In sorting out their own roles in the disease, parents sometimes minimize, rationalize, justify or misrepresent their own adherence to the agreed-upon treatment. Feedback from the other parents helps counter these tendencies.

A Mirror for Self-Discovery

The alternative peer group also provides a mirror for the kids and parents in which to see some of their own behaviors that need to change. When young people share personal issues in a meeting, the ones who are listening begin to look at how those issues may be present in their own lives. The parents, too, will discover ways in which this disease has affected their parenting—and how their parenting has affected the disease—as they hear other parents share their experiences. Our day-to-day behaviors are normally as invisible to us as the air we breathe. As we listen to other parents discuss negative or counterproductive behaviors of their own, we are more able to recognize similar behaviors in ourselves.

Constant Flow of Feedback

Once we gain insight regarding a new behavior we wish to adopt, it is our challenge to make that behavior a habit. If this were easily done, we could read a couple of books on the subject and move on. But it isn't easy. It's very, very hard. One day, we realize it is important to share our feelings with another person, and we do it. The next day, we forget all about it and stay within ourselves and brood. One day, we realize that we have been playing the role of the victim and can point to several recent instances. A week later, we get caught up in blaming others for our situation and have forgotten all about our earlier insight.

In recovery, users and their family members need to learn a number of new behaviors. The other group members help by providing the invaluable service of giving constant feedback to each other. If a young person is justifying or rationalizing, the other kids will point it out. If a parent is minimizing an event or making excuses for his young person's unacceptable behavior, another parent will say so. This constant feedback makes learning new behaviors possible and speeds up the process. Because it is part of the group's dynamic, the kids and parents accept the feedback. This results in continuous—almost painless—intervention.

What Your Young Person Needs To Do

What your young person needs to do will vary over time.

During the first few weeks in the program, your young person needs to attend meetings, coffees and functions. During the first couple weeks, the counselor will be able to determine if your child is or has been using mind-changing chemicals, and whether participating in the program is appropriate for him. As mentioned above, there are some kids who have tried alcohol or marijuana but really don't need to go into a recovery program. Also, there are a few who will need to go directly into an inpatient program.

At your child's first meeting, he will participate in a newcomer's meeting. The meeting leader will be a member of the group who has embraced recovery and has some sobriety. This young person will probably tell the newcomers about his or her own experiences with drugs and recovery. The leader will explain what the program is all about. At meeting's end, the newcomers will have a chance to declare their desire to get clean and sober.

If a newcomer does not want to get sober, he will not be welcome to continue attending meetings.

Wanting to get sober is a program requirement. *Being* sober is not. Many kids who want to get sober do not stick with winners and do not stay sober during their first few weeks in the program. For this reason, newcomers should not hang out with other newcomers unless they have winners with them—usually a member of the Reach Out Committee or the Steering Committee. The counselor can provide a list of winners for newcomers.

Soon after joining the group, the members will be encouraged to get a sponsor and start working a program of recovery. Sponsors will be members of the group who are on their winners list. Each new member will choose someone he likes and wants to learn from. Their sponsors will be their mentors in the program and will help them work on the Twelve Steps of AA. The steps will include writing assignments, reading, lots of sharing and discussion, self-examination and other tasks given by individual sponsors.

What A Parent Can Do During the First Weeks In The Program (The Opening Salvo)

Parents' support of children in the program is vital from the start. As we said earlier, the program only accepts kids who want to get sober. If your young person rejects the program, there are ways to deal with it, and we will address this later in the book.

First, go to meetings. Make a commitment to go to two meetings each week for 30 days. At the end of 30 days, you will have grown accustomed to the meeting format. In meetings you will have the opportunity to share your experience, strength and hope. All are encouraged to contribute. Speakers limit the time of their sharing so that many in the group will get an opportunity to speak. No cross-talk (direct responses to someone else's sharing) or advice-giving is permitted. One-on-one discussions can take place after the meeting, including at the post-meeting coffee.

Everyone reacts differently to the first few meetings. Some parents are comfortable immediately and are greatly relieved to find other parents facing the same problems. For some, the meetings appear to be whining sessions and a waste of time. For some, the level of sharing and intimacy feels inappropriate and embarrassing. This will pass.

Here is the initial reaction of co-author Jennifer Cummings to the meetings:

"I really disliked the parent meetings for the first three months. I only went every other week. I went because the counselor insisted that it was important to my son's recovery. I was disgusted by what appeared to be the parents feeling sorry for themselves and talking about their own problems when we should have been talking about how to fix our kids.

"The first thing I liked about the meetings was that the other parents were so real and open in their sharing. Nowhere else in my life did I get to experience that. Then I started caring about them and their situations. I began to take comfort in knowing people who were going through the same craziness as I was and understood what I was going through. And hearing other parents sharing stories of successes, I began to have faith that my son could get well.

"I don't remember deciding to listen for solutions. But I started learning the parenting skills I needed to support recovery."

If you don't think you are getting much out of meetings after a couple of weeks, try harder. Take notes. Listen for what can be learned from the experiences of the other parents. Far more will be provided to you in the meetings than we can describe in this book.

Besides going to meetings, go to coffee and get to know other parents in the group. Ask for their advice and share your experiences. The parents in the group are very good listeners. And they will learn and grow stronger from listening to you.

Schedule a meeting with the counselor to discuss your child's case and get in-depth information on the program and how it works.

Keep reading and learning all you can about the disease. The parents' role in recovery is critical and there is a tremendous amount to learn and a number of difficult situations for which to prepare. The earlier you learn and the better you learn, the more effective you will be.

Ask questions. Ask questions. Ask questions. Ask questions.

During these early weeks, you don't need to advise your child about sponsors, meetings or the virtues of sticking with winners. If your young person were open to your advice, you wouldn't be in the program in the first place. The counselor and other kids in the group will handle the advice. The best you can do for your young person in this initial period is to step back, trust the group a little and let your child participate.

At this point—if just for now—*consider* letting go and letting God and the group take care of your young person.

4

The Five Horsemen of the A-dope-alypse (What We Are up against)

"To ignore evil is to become an accomplice to it."
— Dr. Martin Luther King, Jr.

To effectively deal with substance abuse and young people, parents must be aware of what we are up against, just how complicated this situation is, and how different cultural elements contribute to it.

There are a few key factors we like to call the "Five Horsemen of the A-dope-alypse," after the four horsemen of the apocalypse from the *Book of Revelations*. These are the five really big obstacles in dealing with young people and substance abuse:

1. The disease of chemical dependency and disease prejudice

2. *Suburbanitus afflluenza*

3. Ethos and societal values

4. The outlaw mindset and self-mythology

5. The family dance

Obstacle No. 1: The Disease and Disease Prejudice

Chemical dependence is a bio-behavioral disease affecting the physiology of the brain and the brain chemistry. The physical changes prompt and motivate a complicated system of justifications, rationalizations, denial and other delusions that lead the sufferer to continue to take the drug. Chemical dependence may have a genetic component. If not treated, the disease is fatal. Death can come quickly through overdose, suicide or car accident, or more slowly through liver disease, sexually transmitted diseases or general physical degeneracy.

Neurology

For years, the treatment community has been using the "disease concept" as a simile. "It is like a disease." "You have to treat it like a disease." Now we have scientific evidence that it is, in fact, a disease. We have information about how the chemistry of the brain changes when mind-changing chemicals are introduced to the body. We also have some evidence as to what happens to the chemistry of the brain immediately after the usage stops, and over time. We have data showing the damage to the brain's neurons caused by certain drugs, and the extent to which the neurons are damaged permanently.

Progressive and Chronic

Chemical dependence is a progressive disease that worsens over time, both during periods of using and of sobriety. It is chronic—once you have the disease, you have it for the rest of your life.

Resistance

This disease is cunning, baffling and powerful. The brain of the person with the disease does not want to be cured. The brain wants the high the drugs provide—and the brain will lie to itself to get it.

Contagion

There is yet another element to this disease: contagion. Not only is it contagious to other young people, its effects spread vertically to parents and grandparents. While the young person is using, the parents are suffering from the disease's ravages, too. The disease takes all of the loving, caring, giving things that parents do and twists them until they not only do not help but can actually hurt the user. Today, we label those intentionally caring behaviors that get abused by the disease as "codependency" and "enabling."

Cure?

There is no known cure for this disease, but we do know what a person can do to put it and keep it in remission. If the user will do these things and keep doing these things, he is almost assured of surviving the disease.

Parent Support

Making the right decisions as parents will be easier if you understand that we are dealing with a disease and not just bad or rebellious behavior. Parents need to take a strong stand in support of treatment just as they would if their child needed radiation therapy or kidney dialysis. This isn't intramural sports or Scouts or getting braces. Treatment is required, and parents need to do whatever it takes to make sure their child undertakes that treatment.

Disease Prejudice

While parents are supporting treatment for their kids, our society, unfortunately, will not be supporting the parents. Medical insurance may provide some financial support of certain treatments for a limited amount of time. Oddly, insurance more often pays for the more costly and less effective treatments, such as 30-day hospital stays. Insurance companies also will pay for emergency treatment for an overdose. Fewer pay for less expensive outpatient services. Treatment for substance abuse is covered at a lower level (insurance pays for a lower percentage of the costs) and there are separate lifetime limits. This is because our society as a whole does not yet accept that chemical dependency is a disease. Our society still treats chemical dependency as a moral or character problem. This is what we call "disease prejudice." We who have chemically dependent children know now that their affliction really is a disease, but our larger society does not treat the problem like a disease.

Imagine the public's panic if this disease were accompanied by an ulcer in the middle of the forehead. How many parents would attend meetings about the disease in that case? If hundreds of thousands of young people across the nation had this ulcer on their foreheads, what would our lawmakers and media be doing? It would be better for all of us if this disease did include an ulcer on the forehead, because then we would all be taking the necessary actions to fight the disease.

Obstacle No. 2: Suburbanitus Affluenza

 "Material abundance without character is the surest way to destruction."

—Thomas Jefferson

The second obstacle in dealing with young people and substance abuse is what I call *suburbanitus affluenza*. Many young people have a lot given to them and do very little on their own to earn it. "Suburbanitus affluenza" has to do with what a person has versus what he has produced on his own. Having a lot of physical possessions and an affluent lifestyle feeds the ego. Being able to produce through your own efforts is a statement of self-esteem. The problem is that if a young person's ego rises high while the self-esteem remains low, it's hard for him to quit using drugs and alcohol.

In our culture today, it is easier for most parents to give more material goods and privileges to their children and harder to stand by requiring the children to go without unless they've earned the rewards on their own through outside work or family chores. Often, parents who sense that their children are suffering from low self-esteem will feel guilty that they haven't given them enough, and so shower them with more goodies, even if the parents can't comfortably afford to buy them.

The truth is that most of us do not need our young people to help financially support the family. Our children do not get to be important to the family in that way. We don't even need them to help at home by doing chores. If we haven't raised them from a young age to help, we find it's easier to do the housework ourselves or to hire outside help.

This lack of connection between being given what one needs and wants without having earned the rewards through one's own efforts can contribute to an individual's deep level of anxiety. Not only is the young person not learning that he can produce these tangible results through his or her own efforts, but the cars, clothes and lifestyle on which the child's identity is based is not something that he can control.

A large percentage of young people are enjoying the fruits of a lifestyle provided by parents who are highly trained professionals, highly skilled workers and/or successful entrepreneurs; but the children themselves do not even know if they would be able to hold down a job at McDonald's. These young people may not be thinking about this, but on some level they are aware of this disconnection, and carry anxiety from not knowing how it will be resolved.

This lack of work also leads to excessive leisure time. If kids are successfully channeled into healthy, time-consuming, extracurricular activities, they likely won't face this problem. If they are not, however, they'll grow bored and seek other diversions.

Obstacle No. 3: Ethos and Societal Values

Ethos is defined as the fundamental character or spirit of a culture; the underlying sentiment that informs the beliefs, customs, or practices of a society. It is a thread of a culture's historical, long-held beliefs. In the United States, we don't have much ethos. Immigrant groups have brought with them the ethos of their home cultures, which have died away or been absorbed into our culture.

To study a culture's ethos, one can examine its myths. Myths are stories a people holds on to over long periods of time, if they fit in with the people's beliefs. Our nation is relatively young and we arguably haven't yet to produce our own myths. What we do have are legends: American tall tales. In these tales we generally find bigger-than-life characters such as Pecos Bill, Paul Bunyan and John Henry. These are rugged, self-reliant individuals, pull-yourself-up-by-the-bootstraps characters. This presents a contradiction to our children. Our culture says that we value education, yet we glorify those who have made it without being handed the benefit of an education.

This contradiction shows up in our culture today in whom we celebrate and publicize. Sometimes we idolize a very successful businessman, but only if he made it on his own, pioneering a company or industry, such as Bill Gates. Otherwise, our heroes run to entertainment personalities: actors, rock 'n' roll stars or multimillionaire athletes.

We don't mean to, but we are sending double messages to our kids. We say that we value hard work and a good education, but we glamorize people who make it without the benefits of education. We say that we value sexual responsibility, but the only Miss America who has recently become an enduring celebrity in the national spotlight gained her sustaining fame after *Penthouse* published nude photographs of her. We say not to do drugs, that you can't be successful if you smoke dope. But the 42nd president of the United States did as a young man, and his successor was arrested for driving drunk And one of our most popular singers, Willie Nelson, bragged about smoking pot in the White House.

Our belief system is wacky. All of these mixed values are being passed on to our kids. And they are passed on in indirect ways. They aren't presented to our children for their consideration. They are being passed on in unconscious ways that bypass critical thinking. Play by the rules, we say. But children also see those who strayed from following the rules, and went on to ever greater success.

Obstacle No. 4: The Outlaw Mindset and Self-Mythology

If you have ever consciously broken the law, you know that one of the necessary ingredients to breaking a rule is rationalizing why it's OK. If you ask a prison inmate whether he did the act that he was put in prison for, and if he is honest with you, he will say yes and then explain why. He will provide a great reason. He will have a justification and a rationalization.

When you are suffering from *suburbanitus affluenza,* and you have a disease that says that any time you feel uncomfortable you can make the feeling go away instantly by taking a chemical, and you have dual messages from your culture about the consequences of doing your own thing, and all you have standing in your way is that it's against the law to use drugs, it is easy to develop a self-mythology about why it is OK to break that law.

John Cates (this book's co-author):
"*I was a suburban kid who became a functioning addict. We weren't rich or poor. There was nothing in my background which pointed to my becoming an addict. I was raised going to church and learned about a grace-filled loving God. I was taught a work ethic. When I was using drugs, I worked. While I was at college in the early '70s, I went from smoking dope to shooting heroin. I graduated from college and started teaching*

school while I was shooting heroin. I was really cool—I had long hair and got to school on a motorcycle. (That was when we said that just because you have long hair doesn't mean you are getting high. That was a lie. If you had long hair, chances were really good you were getting high.) I was still shooting heroin when I was serving on the professional ethics committee of the teacher's association.

"So how could I justify and rationalize this? I drew on the example of Francis Marion, 'The Swamp Fox.' He was a Revolutionary War hero, made famous by Disney, who taught school in colonial America by day and smuggled rum past the British at night. I was a schoolteacher by day; at night I was a guerrilla fighter. That's what I saw myself as. Is that insane? But it worked. It was the oppressive government trying to keep us from what was our right—they allow alcohol, they should let us use heroin. That is an example of a self-mythology. It lets us rationalize and justify what we want to do."

A lot of the kids come into the recovery program having adopted a self-mythology of being "bad-ass," a gangster. There is plenty of support for this fantasy in music and videos today. These kids will have built their identity around this.

To get well, these kids will have to own up to the reality that they chose that identity. Then they can elect new self-mythologies, as well as replace the outlaw mindset with a new one. The new self-mythologies will be in harmony with the new mindset and will give their egos an identity that doesn't conflict with living a principle-based life.

Obstacle No. 5: The Family Dance

The family is so powerful in a young person's life. Parents of drug-using teenagers believe they have lost control and have no influence over their son or daughter. But the truth is that what the family does to address the disease is probably the most important determinant of whether the child will get well.

You have probably heard the expression, "There's an elephant in the room." Before substance abuse is addressed, everyone in the family is affected by this "elephant," but pretends it isn't going on. Imagine an elephant in the living room with everyone walking around it and climbing over it, and you will have a vision of the "dance" when the family is operating in denial.

When one person in the family is affected by addiction, it affects everyone else. When a young person is acting out his disease, the parents are horribly saddened and afraid. The father might respond to his fear with over-reactive anger. The mother may make excuses and cover up to avoid unpleasantness. The siblings experience anxiety and confusion. The family's responses usually feed the disease. The young person with the disease will use one parent's over-reactive anger as a reason to justify breaking the rules and abandoning the parents' values. The child will use the other parent's over-protection to avoid consequences. The parents may turn to workaholism or other busy-ness to avoid feelings of fear and anxiety about what is happening. This will help the user avoid detection and consequences awhile longer. Meanwhile, the parents are not emotionally present for the other children in the family, who may start acting out, as well, or lying low and repressing their feelings. If the user feels guilt about the misery he is causing his family, he will use drugs to avoid those feelings, as well.

In short, the family's initial response to substance abuse is usually some kind of craziness that supports the disease.

Fortunately, the family also can be a powerful tool of recovery. And while unhealthy family dynamics are tangled and complex, the principles for a helpful and healthy family dynamic are simple.

5

Using Recovery Tools

"I have a new philosophy. I'm only going to dread one day at a time."

—Charles M. Schulz, creator of the comic strip *Peanuts*

In early recovery, addicts need to learn the basic tools of Twelve-Step recovery. They learn it in the meetings and while hanging out with the other kids in the program. For some kids, their recovery work is supplemented by one-on-one or group counseling within the program. In second-stage recovery, they learn the concepts of recovery on a deeper level and how to apply them to broader areas of their lives, such as dating, family, school and work.

We describe some of the tools of recovery below, along with suggestions for parents.

Meetings

Meetings are gatherings of people in recovery at which participants share their experience, strength and hope. There is a typical format for most meetings. The group holds hands while someone reads the opening, a statement of the purpose of the program, and leads the group in a moment of silence. Then the meeting leader welcomes the group. There is a reading of the Twelve Steps, and a designated member presents a topic. The meeting is then opened up for the other members to speak and share their feelings and thoughts. The meeting closes with the famous serenity prayer: "God grant me the serenity to accept the things I cannot change, courage to change the things I can, and wisdom to know the difference."

The benefits of meetings are many for the addict. In meetings, children learn to trust others and accept their support. Sharing feelings is therapeutic. Once feelings are shared, they lose their power over the person. Sharing an experience also has the effect of putting that experience in perspective. Listening provides similar gifts. When the addict hears her own feeling (or issue) expressed by someone else, she is then able to distinguish that feeling (or issue) in herself. Before this, it may have been running her and she didn't even know it was there. She can relate to the person who shared the feeling (or issue), and can deal with it from looking at it from the outside.

Imagine the relief a teenager feels when he hears another teenager share his feelings about not being accepted by other kids and how important that is to him. Imagine what getting honest about those feelings can do to empower him in making better decisions. When he hears how one of his peers has learned to deal with feelings of rejection, then learned to relate to other kids in a positive way, he can see that as a possibility for himself.

Meetings also provide a means, other than drugs, to manage anxiety. Meetings produce a biochemical effect. When a person shares feelings in a meeting, his anxiety level goes down.

You can support recovery by requiring that your young person go to meetings. Going to meetings is something we know increases the probability of living through the disease of addiction.

And go to meetings yourself—to parent meetings. Parents come into the group weighed down by feelings of sadness, guilt, anger, fear and hopelessness. Parents come in suffering from extreme anxiety about their children. This anxiety becomes a tool of the disease, actually working against recovery. When parents are suffering from anxiety, they want to do anything to relieve the anxiety and not do anything that will increase it. A parent in the throes of anxiety may act out of that feeling instead of a higher commitment to do the things and take the stands that will help the young person recover. In the midst of severe anxiety, our ability to make wise decisions is impaired. Going to meetings helps manage that anxiety.

To repeat, there is a biochemical effect from sharing at meetings: the chemistry of the brain is affected, decreasing anxiety. In turn, we can become wiser and more effective in helping our children into strong recovery.

Just as for the kids, there are other benefits parents can reap from attending meetings. By listening to other parents in the group, parents learn to distinguish patterns that are contributing to their children's addiction and inhibiting recovery. We can usually distinguish these patterns in others pretty clearly before we can begin to notice them in ourselves. Also, through attending meetings, parents get in touch with their feelings in a way that is relieving and empowering. When we are not aware of our feelings, our feelings can run us.

Finally, parents learn from other parents what works to combat the disease and what does not; what is going on in the child's group; and what other resources are available.

Important Benefits of Regular and Frequent Attendance at Parent Meetings

1. **Education: General and specific to each family**

2. **Accountability**

3. **Manipulation inoculation**

4. **Alternative offerings, planning, evaluation**

5. **Personal support**

6. **Personal introspection opportunities**

| 7. | **Acquisition of extra resources** |

Meeting etiquette is simple. There is little or no cross-talk. Each sharing is more or less related to the topic; but the topic does not become a discussion in and of itself. There is no giving of advice. Parents can ask for advice after the meeting. If someone has not asked for advice, it is better not to give it. It is recommended, for anxiety-control purposes, that you share at every meeting—but you are welcome to merely sit and listen. Sometimes, one member of the group will have a lot to share at a particular meeting. Once in awhile it will be the right thing to share at some length. At most meetings, each member should only speak briefly so that most members get a chance to share. If you have more to share, or if you don't get the opportunity, look for someone to share with one-on-one after the meeting. Doing so will be helpful for the person you share with, as well as for yourself.

Sponsorship

Young people are encouraged to ask a same-sex person in the group to be their sponsor. Each chooses a group member with some sobriety and from whom the child would be willing to learn. The child's sponsor will coach him through the Twelve Steps. The child is encouraged to call the sponsor on a regular basis to check in, to discuss feelings and thoughts and get support. The sponsor will help the child learn the tools of recovery.

In recovery, the addict needs to learn to trust someone other than himself because his own thoughts are not reliable. Because he has this disease, his own brain will lie to him in order to get the drugs it craves. The sponsor is someone the addict chooses to trust over his own brain. The sponsor will have some responsibility for confronting the addict and holding him accountable for his actions. The sponsor relationship is controlled by the addict. The addict chooses the sponsor, the addict calls the sponsor. It is not a care-taking relationship.

You can best support your young person's sponsor/sponsored relationship by staying out of it. Your son or daughter will not learn to trust and open up to the sponsor if the sponsor is reporting to, or collaborating with, you. (An exception to this rule exists in situations where special accountability systems are needed. The counselor can help direct the parameters of this specialized relationship.)

You should get a sponsor for yourself. Modeling this for the addict supports the process. More importantly, parents need all the support they can get to stand up to the disease. They need someone they can trust to discuss the day-to-day decisions that need to be made. They need someone to guide them through the Twelve Steps and to learn the tools of recovery. They need to have the benefit of a person to whom they have given permission to confront and advise them. As mentioned earlier, the addict's decisions may be led by pervading feelings of anxiety. Similarly, a parent's decisions may be influenced by anxiety, and a sponsor can provide calm during the storm. A parent's sponsor is the parent's private tutor and friend. Most parent sponsors will give the sponsored permission to call whenever the need arises (often the need arises late at night). The sponsored, in turn, should invite the sponsor to be honest and open and to hold the parent accountable.

Hint: When you pick a sponsor, you should choose another member of the parent group who has something you want. Keep it simple. It may be a greater spirituality, or knowledge of how to parent an addicted child, or knowledge of the Twelve Steps. It should be someone you like and respect. When in doubt, you can ask someone to be your temporary sponsor. Don't procrastinate by looking for your own St. Francis or Mahatma Gandhi.

Owning Behavior

A key concept in early recovery is ownership—owning one's own feelings, abilities, decisions and behaviors.

As long as it is something or someone else's fault, the addict is powerless to change his situation. But any behavior or situation he owns, he has power over. For example, if Beth thinks she failed a school test because the material was too hard and her teacher can't teach, she will keep failing. The material *will* appear to be too hard, and trying to pass it pointless. But if Beth thinks she failed the test because she didn't study enough, or because she didn't ask for help, then she has the power to choose to study enough and ask for help. If she got drunk last night because her boyfriend broke up with her, or her parents were mean to her, or her friends wouldn't hang out with her, or because her dog died, then she will be powerless over alcohol when she gets a ticket, or fails a test, or has a bad hair day. But if she can own that she got drunk last night because she chose to take that first drink, or she chose to hang out with kids who were drinking, or she chose not to call her sponsor when she started thinking about going out with those friends, then she can see that she is not driven by forces outside of herself—*she has the power to make different choices.*

Without owning behavior, the addict cannot recover. An addict must learn to make the right choices in the face of any feelings and circumstances.

Parents can help by letting their young person own his behavior. No matter what happened in their home that evening, it is the addict who chose to either use a drug or to reach out to someone who could be supportive. The parents should not make excuses for their children. It does not make it easier for them to recover. It teaches them to look outside themselves where they can place blame. *The addict* chose not to study. *The addict* chose to disregard the traffic laws. *The addict* chose to use. Hearing that from the parent is empowering, even if this thought line is new and, therefore, uncomfortable. Holding the addict accountable for his actions is not for the purpose of making him wrong. Holding people accountable helps them get in touch with reality from an empowering position.

As a parent, you can teach the concept of owning behavior by owning *your* own behavior. Modeling can accelerate the addict's learning. "I was in a hurry and chose to speed. Now I have to pay a ticket." "I got mad and said things that led to my sister not wanting to talk to me." You can own behavior toward your young person without letting him off the hook. You can make amends for what you did tonight or two years ago without taking on responsibility for the choices your son or daughter has made.

The following are some examples of not owning and of owning feelings or behavior:

Being a Victim (not owning)	Owning Feelings/Behavior
I don't tell my husband because he just gets mad and loses his temper. (The situation is such that I can't tell my husband these things.)	I didn't tell my husband because I was afraid that he would lose his temper, and I get scared when that happens. (I chose not to tell my husband. Next time I may choose to tell him even though it makes me uncomfortable.)
I'm late because traffic was bad.	I'm late because I didn't allow time for a traffic jam.
I don't have a father; he left when I was little. He doesn't care about me and I don't care about him.	I have a father but I'm choosing not to have a relationship with him right now.
I can't be happy until I know my children are happy.	I love my children and want the best for them. And I am choosing to demonstrate my devotion by withholding good things from myself while my children are in trouble. I am responsible for my own happiness and will work toward it despite what happens to the people I love.
I can't handle this, it makes me crazy.	I am scared of making the wrong decision and alienating my child.

The following are examples of letting the addict off the hook, versus holding him accountable (that is, letting him own his own behavior).

Making Excuses/Letting him off the hook	Holding the Addict Accountable
It's my fault, I wasn't there to support you when you needed it.	I'm sorry that I didn't spend more time with you. But you are the one who chose to use drugs. (Implied: the child has the power to make positive decisions for himself despite what his family life is like.)
You were supposed to get a job this week but you had a lot of things come up that made it difficult, so you can have another two weeks to find a job.	It is a principle of this family that everyone gainfully works full-time or goes to school full-time or does both part-time. You have chosen full-time work and you had until today to find a job. You didn't find one. The following natural consequences will entail until you are employed . . .
We gave you money for your expenses to last until the end of the month and it's gone after two weeks. We can't let you starve so here is some more money—but make it last.	You have no money left for the rest of the month. How do you plan to eat?

These responses may seem to tough, but they honor the strength and capabilities that the addict does possess. When the addict owns his behavior and the consequences of his behavior, he is motivated and empowered to find within himself the qualities he needs to develop the ability to make good decisions and manage his behavior.

In addition to owning behavior, young people in recovery and their parents need to own their emotions. Most of us confuse ourselves by denying, mislabeling and stuffing the emotions we are feeling. Before choosing an action to take, it is a good idea not only to identify a feeling, but to accept that we are feeling that way.

To help a child in recovery, each parent needs to own his own feelings. Parents may come into recovery in misery and despair because their young person is using drugs, but their misery and despair are not the fault of the user—children are not responsible for their parents' feelings. Parents also need to own their feelings about their parenting. They need to become aware of how much their identity is defined by how they see themselves as a parent. Many parents come into the program miserable because they can't stand feeling like failures as parents. They need to learn to own their feelings so that they can be aware of when and why they are making decisions. Are their decisions motivated by feelings, such as fear, worry, loneliness and anxiety? Decisions should be made based on the realities of the situation and reason.

Owning their feelings also will accelerate the learning process. Many fathers entering the program are almost paralyzed with what they identify or perceive as anger. Some fathers are so angry that they can't make friends with possible allies who can help them fight the disease. What these fathers are really feeling is, usually, fear, sometimes guilt (unwarranted), or shame. When they can identify these feelings, admit and accept them, it takes the power out of them. Then they can take part in the procedures that will help to save their children.

By owning their own feelings, parents serve as role models for their kids, which will make it easier for the kids to learn to own their own feelings. Also, when parents stop putting inappropriate responsibility on their young people for how the parents feel, the young person is relieved of feeling responsible for the impossible task of managing the parents' feelings.

If owning your own feelings is an issue for you, then this is one of the opportunities you have to make a major change that will open the door to other healthy changes for your family, which will surely follow. And it is totally within your power.

Sticking with Winners

We discussed the importance of "sticking with winners" in Chapter Three. In the earliest days of recovery, the group and/or counselor will help the addict develop a "winners list" of kids he should hang out with. Later in recovery, the young person will develop this list.

What the parents can do is insist that their child sticks with winners. Most young people are not going to want to do it. If the parents insist they do it, their chances of surviving the disease are very high. If they do not, the chances are very, very small. The counselors can provide the parents with a copy of a winners list for their young person. The counselors also can usually tell the parents if the young person is or is not sticking with winners.

As a parent of a young person in recovery, you will benefit by sticking with winners, as well. You don't have to allow family or friends to come to your house and drink. You don't have to take your young person to the homes of relatives where alcohol will be served. And, you can make faster progress learning how to parent children with substance-abuse problems by spending time with other parents in recovery. These are the people who can show the way, who can offer the best support, and who will hold you accountable (if you ask them to).

Finally, you also can be a winner for your recovering young person. By going to meetings and working a program, you model the new behaviors your young person needs to learn. By not having alcohol in your home, or not drinking while your child is in early recovery, you can demonstrate life without using. You can create an environment of change and growth, with a clear stand against the use of alcohol and drugs.

Safety Net

Young people in the program work on creating a safety net of people who will hold them accountable to their program of recovery. If they surround themselves with "winners," they will have this safety net.

They learn to use their safety net when they are experiencing negative feelings or temptations to take actions that can lead to relapse.

As a parent you cannot do anything to help your young person create this safety net. You can create one for yourself by getting to know the other parents in the group. Call them on the phone, go to coffee and attend functions. If you do these things, over a short period of time the other parents will become a tremendous resource for you.

The Twelve Steps of AA

The Twelve Steps pioneered by Alcoholics Anonymous provide mental and emotional suggestions that lead to actions. The Steps give a structure for learning the skills and behaviors necessary to treat the disease.

Working the Twelve Steps is not the only way to get and stay sober. But for many people, following The Steps is helpful, and for many it is critical. For the sufferer, working The Steps leads to getting and maintaining sobriety. For loved ones, it leads to becoming effective agents in combating the disease, and to attaining and maintaining health and energy for the task.

Working The Steps means working them as a whole, as well as individually. You need to talk to your sponsor about how to work The Steps into your recovery program.

Acting 'As If'

A big breakthrough in AA was the idea of acting oneself into thinking, or acting "as if." Alcoholics used to wait for their feelings and thoughts to get OK and then stop using. Out of desperation, some sufferers started taking certain actions first, and this led to staying sober. Living a commitment to take certain actions protects the addict from the trickery of the brain—the justification and rationalization and other means of mis-thinking ourselves into patterns of living that lead to using. In the program, acting "as if" is also termed, "Fake it till you make it".

This skill is important for parents as well as children. Whether you have faith in the recovery process, choose a sponsor and start working the Twelve Steps. Whether you feel like it or not, go to meetings. The rest will follow.

Humility

To have humility is to be teachable. It is admitting that you don't know it all and you can't do it all by yourself. If you have humility, you are open to learning new things and can accept the support of others. When young people learn humility, they become open to learning the tools of recovery. They understand that humility is a strength, not a weakness; an asset, not a character flaw.

The opposite of having humility is being hardheaded, arrogant. It's hard to teach people anything if they believe they already know it all and are afraid to find out they don't. For this reason, the most intelligent people can be the most difficult to reach.

You can support your young person in attaining humility by modeling it. Become teachable, and let it show. If you can't do that, then just be willing to entertain the possibility that you could have something to learn.

Tough Love

Tough love is a juggling act. It is the process of keeping two balls in the air: solid, sincere, loving boundaries; and delivery of the message of unconditional love, even as you say "no."

Most parents are good at one ball, but not the other. Parents who are good at the "tough ball" are usually afraid of being too lenient. Parents who are good at the "love ball" are afraid of being too hard. Whatever you are afraid of is indicative of which ball you deal with best. Knowing this, you'll know which ball you need to work on to become effective as a parent.

Building A Relationship with a Higher Power

In order to get and stay sober, the young person needs to develop a relationship with a power she recognizes to be greater than herself. This co-author, as a counselor, has been doing this work for more than 20 years, and I have been exposed to more than 50,000 cases. And I have never known anyone with long-term sobriety who did not establish a regular, practical relationship with God. Much could be said about why this is the case. But it doesn't matter. It is a fact, and it is a gift of addiction and recovery.

The best thing you can do as a parent to support your young person in developing a relationship with a higher power is to develop your relationship with *your* higher power. Having a strong spiritual life will give you serenity and clarity, which in turn will enable you to make wise decisions and give you the strength to see them through.

6

Leaving Orbit

If you have been centered around your child's life for a long time, your life has probably become like the surface of the moon—barren and dreary. This is the natural result of spending years circling around someone else, getting hit with things that leave holes, and gathering dust.

In earlier chapters, we have told you that your child's addiction is not your fault. This is true. However, how you parent your child during his recovery can make a tremendous difference in whether he makes it. You can create an environment that supports change and personal growth. And there is no end to how far you can take this.

If you want to maximize your contribution, then go on a search for where you can make a difference. This chapter will give you some ideas. But you will need to turn your focus on yourself and your life.

You can begin by committing to working your own program of recovery. Ah . . . but *you* are not the addict. Have I mentioned that this is a family disease? If your spouse or child is abusing drugs or alcohol, or has some other addiction, then you need to work a program.

If your spouse or child is abusing drugs or alcohol or has some other addiction, then you need to work your own program of recovery.

Your wellbeing is equally as important as your child's. Also, your wellbeing will contribute astonishingly to your child's. Our families operate like mobiles, those sculptures of carefully balanced parts that are often found over the dentist's chair. When one part moves, all the others begin to move—maintaining a balance with each other. It is exciting when you first see this happening in your own family. Perhaps you already can see this process in your own family. Perhaps you are considering working a program because of the changes that your child already has made.

You should work a program for yourself, but I promise you that for every positive change you make in your life, it will create positive effects within each of the members of your family. Oddly, many parents report that it even affects members of the family they do not have contact with. This is a mystery we cannot explain.

If you are not an addict or alcoholic, then find another issue to work a program on. Consider work-aholism, codependency, overeating, sex addiction, over-spending or low self-esteem. Ask the counselor for some suggestions. Get a sponsor and talk to your sponsor about issues you might address. If you really can't come up with anything at all, then try working a program on denial.

Ask another parent in the program to be your sponsor. If you have a sponsor in another program of recovery, we recommend that you also get a sponsor in this program. Choose someone you would like to learn from, someone who has something that you want (perhaps a child who got sober and is doing well).

If you are a man, choose another father in the group to be your sponsor. If you are a woman, choose one of the other mothers. The sponsor relationship is an intimate one. The more you can share with your sponsor, the more you will gain. Having an opposite-sex partner tends to limit the level of sharing and could lead to an inappropriate relationship.

If you want a sponsor but aren't sure whom to ask, then ask someone to be your temporary sponsor. This person will help you get started while you are getting to know the other parents better.

Once you have a sponsor, talk to the sponsor often. Call often. Most sponsors will leave it to you to reach out to them. This is because you are responsible for your own recovery. It is not because your sponsor doesn't care about you.

For Parents Who Are NOT Codependent

Congratulations. If you are not a codependent then your life has probably not become unmanageable because of your child's addictive behavior. You are not obsessed with controlling your child's behavior and you do not let their behavior overly affect you. And there is a set of behaviors you are not doing that would otherwise work against your young person's recovery.

It may be helpful, however, to consider the possibility that you have at least a few codependent behaviors. By virtue of your being a parent, it would really be extraordinary for you not to have any of these tendencies. And if you can identify even one, it will give you the power to effect change in your family, and serve as a tool to support your child's recovery.

In Melody Beattie's best-selling book, *Codependent No More: How to Stop Controlling Others and Start Caring for Yourself*, she provides a checklist of more than 200 characteristics of codependents. We recommend that you read that book, or at least the following checklist, and see if you don't recognize yourself. Ask yourself the following questions, which are based on Beattie's checklist:

- Do you think and feel responsible for other people or their feelings, thoughts, actions, choices, wants, needs, wellbeing, lack of wellbeing?

- Do you feel anxiety, pity and guilt when other people have a problem?

- Do you feel compelled to help someone else solve their problems, such as offering unwanted advice, giving a rapid-fire series of suggestions, or trying to fix their feelings?

- Do you anticipate other people's needs?

- Do you say yes when you don't want to and do things you don't really want to, do more than your fair share of the work, or things other people are capable of doing for themselves?

- Do you abandon your routine to do something for somebody else or because you are so upset about somebody?

- Do you believe other people are making you crazy?

- Do you feel guilty about spending money on yourself or doing unnecessary or fun things for yourself?

- Do you expect yourself to do everything perfectly?

- Do you try to help other people live their lives instead of living your own?

- Do you lose sleep over problems or other people's behavior?

- Do you try to catch people in acts of misbehavior?

- Do you abandon your routine because they are so upset about somebody or something?

- Do you try to control events and people through helplessness, guilt, coercion, threats, advice-giving, manipulation, or domination?

- Do you pretend circumstances aren't as bad as they are?

- Do you stay at work or stay busy so you don't have to think about things?

- Have you become a workaholic, compulsive spender or gambler, or overeater?

- Have you been looking for happiness outside of yourself?

- Do you center your life around other people?

- Do you say you aren't going to tolerate certain behaviors from other people, and then gradually increase your tolerance until you tolerate things you said you never would?

If you are feeling brave, ask someone who knows you to evaluate you on the issues above. You may be unaware. (In denial?)

If you can relate to any of the characteristics listed above, please read the next section and take from it whatever you can.

For Parents Who **ARE** *Codependents*

Most parents—maybe all parents—have some of the behaviors that characterize codependency. Beattie's book defines codependency this way:

> *A codependent person is one who has let another person's behavior affect him, and who is obsessed with controlling that person's behavior.*

The bad news is that if you are codependent, you have developed a pattern of coping with life that is not healthy for yourself and is detrimental to your young person's recovery.

The good news is that recognizing codependent behaviors gives you the power to change them. And changing those behaviors sets up a domino effect of change in the family that supports recovery.

Consider some typical codependent behavior and how it affects your young person.

Codependent Behavior	Effect on Your Addicted Child
Giving advice or suggestions, or trying to fix feelings to solve your child's problems.	Feels incompetent to solve his or her own problems. Thinks that eventually someone else will solve them.
Pretending circumstances aren't as bad as they are—denial.	Feels confused. Thinks the circumstances aren't as bad as they are—denial.
Lying to protect and cover up for your child's behavior.	Not held accountable. Does not experience natural consequences.
Tolerating behaviors you said you would not tolerate.	Not held accountable. Enabled in addictive behaviors.
Not taking care of yourself.	Learns not to take care of himself.
Sacrificing your happiness while obsessing on saving your child's life.	Feelings of guilt that are numbed through the addictive behavior.

How have codependent behaviors worked for you? One parent described it this way:

"It was like trying to drive a car from the passenger seat. For all my efforts, I didn't have the power to set the direction of my son's life or to stop him. I focused all of my energy on fixing what I was powerless to fix, and my own life became unmanageable. I didn't take care of my life except through him. I thought that if only he would be happy, I would be happy. He was my focus. I just didn't realize how deadly my focus was."

Now consider the effect on your child when your behavior changes.

New Parental Behavior	Effect on Your Addicted Child
Letting your child own his own problems and feelings.	Feels empowered. Realizes that if his life is going to work out, he will have to do the work. No one will do it for him. He doesn't need someone else to do it for him.
Being honest about the problems.	Feels less comfortable about the state of his life. Not as comfortable that things can keep going on as they are.
Not covering up for your child's behavior.	Gets to experience the natural consequences of his behavior.
Setting definite and clear limits that you insist upon being respected if your child is to live in your home.	Gets the benefit of some externally provided limits on his behavior. If he chooses to overstep the limits set, he gets to experience the consequences.
Taking care of yourself. Taking responsibility for your own feelings.	Learns, by example, healthy behaviors for dealing with feelings and the concept of taking responsibility for his own wellbeing.
Focusing on enjoying your own life. Not focusing on saving your child.	Relieved of the guilt of being responsible for your unhappiness. Realizes that no one else will take on the responsibility of getting his life on track.

By getting out of the way, your young person can begin to manage his own life. By not protecting him, the discomfort caused by the natural consequences of addiction can work in his favor. By giving him responsibility for his life and the consequences of his choices, your young person is empowered.

Beattie has written several excellent books on codependency, including: *Codependent No More; Beyond Codependency;* and, *Codependents' Guide to the Twelve Steps.* We highly recommend reading one or more of these books. She has also written a day-by-day book, which has been popular with parents of young people in recovery, *The Language of Letting Go.*

Having Fun

It is easier for many of us to be martyrs than to have fun. When we have a serious problem, we take it seriously and don't have time for fun. And if we are suffering, fun seems like an impossibility. But fun isn't impossible in the midst of suffering, and it actually contributes to the solution.

Schedule fun and pleasure in your life every week. It will clear your head so that you will be able to make better decisions. Imagine a chalkboard that is used every day for years but never gets erased. After you can't read the white chalk any longer, you use yellow, and then blue, and then green, until everything is an indecipherable mess. That's what our minds get like when we don't give it real breaks through fun and relaxation. Each belly laugh will clean part of the chalkboard for you. With regular fun, you will regain perspective and clarity of mind.

Setting Boundaries

Learning to set clear boundaries is an important tool for making your life manageable and supporting your child's recovery. You need to separate what is yours and what is not. No amount of effort will make you successful at being responsible for your young person's life. You are responsible *to* your children, not *for* them. You are responsible for *your* feelings, not your spouse's feelings. What is yours to manage, God has given you the power to manage.

Only you can determine what your boundaries are going to be. And it is an ongoing process. The discussion below will help you get started.

Parents in the program must, early on, address two particular boundaries: what will and will not be tolerated in the family home; and what kind of treatment the parents will and will not accept from their young person. Parents need to state their stand on these issues and administer consequences if their boundaries are crossed.

No Abuse of Persons Given or Accepted

There can be a lot of variability in boundaries from family to family. But there is one basic rule that every family should have—no physical or verbal abuse. You should not let yourself be treated badly in this way. It does not empower or protect your children to allow anything of this kind. And it will hurt them in many ways. They will feel shame for doing it. They will respect you and themselves less, so it will hurt their self-esteem. And it will allow them to be out of control, taking away an opportunity to learn self-control and acceptable behavior. If your child physically or verbally abuses you or anyone else in the family, the consequence should probably be for the child to live somewhere else for a period of time.

> **Accepting mistreatment from your young person hurts your young person's self-esteem. It does not support him in any way.**

If you don't know whether certain behavior is abusive, talk to the counselor or someone else whose judgment you trust.

Personal Space and Property

Another boundary area is the use and care of property. What is yours, theirs or the whole family's? We already have discussed the issue of the child's bedroom. In most cases, we suggest you let her room be her space. That means that it can be messy. That means that, unless you think she is hiding drugs, you respect her privacy and don't look through the things she keeps in the room. What is in her room and how messy or clean she keeps it is her prerogative and responsibility.

Who are your kids allowed to have in your house? And when? You have a right not to allow into your home people you don't like or trust. And you have a right to set curfews as to when guests can be over. It also is your responsibility to set those boundaries.

There are subtler boundary issues that, when clarified, will make your lives more manageable. These are boundaries that separate you from others. For example, your feelings and others' feelings. Your feelings are yours and are your responsibility. To be healthy and effective as a parent, you need to recognize your feelings, own them and manage them.

> **To be an effective parent, you need to recognize your feelings, own them and manage them.**

Owning Your Feelings

Learning to recognize your own feelings may take time and help from your sponsor or a counselor. It may take intervention from your friends or your sponsor for you to become aware of where you are not recognizing your own feelings. You can facilitate this process by asking yourself often what you are feeling, and writing it down. It also helps to talk about your feelings to others.

Identifying your feelings puts you in a position to own your feelings. If you know you feel anxious, you can do the things that you have learned will reduce your anxiety. This may be talking to other parents, praying, getting exercise, identifying your areas of responsibility and taking care of them, or identifying the things you are not responsible for and giving them to God to take care of.

Other parents, your sponsor, or a counselor or therapist may be able to help you identify your feelings. They also may be able to give you some suggestions for dealing with them. But no one but you can take responsibility for them and manage them.

Helping Your Young Person to Own Feelings

Likewise, your young person has her own feelings that she can learn to identify, own and manage. Her feelings are not your responsibility. If she should ask you to help her deal with her feelings (not likely), you may have some advice to give her. However, unless she asks for your input, you should respect her boundaries and let her have and manage her own feelings. To do otherwise would be invasive and would be crossing her boundaries. Also, it would serve to delay her learning process.

Your child can manage her own feelings. She can bear her own fears and disappointments, just as you have in your life. Are there exceptions? Yes. Rarely, but sometimes, a young person takes his or her own life. If your child is talking about suicide, you need to put her in the hospital. If your child is not talking about suicide, and if your child is connected to other young people in the group, or to the counselor, then you don't need to monitor the nuances of her feelings.

The best thing you can do to help your young person with boundary issues is to model them. It is OK for you to talk about your own feelings and what you are doing to manage them as long as you are not crossing another parent/child boundary by sharing too much, expecting your young person to solve your problems.

Sharing Too Much

There are areas of life that parents should not share with their children—for example, most issues related to the parent's sexuality. Some parents, perhaps because their own boundaries were crossed as a child, do not know this. Crossing parent/child boundaries inappropriately with regard to sexuality, even verbally, is incest. If your parents crossed these boundaries with you, you would do well to discuss this with a counselor or therapist. And you should really reach out for help in establishing the proper boundaries with your own children. If your boundaries were crossed, you probably won't be able to set healthy boundaries without outside help.

Looking to your young person for emotional support can be another form of incest, called emotional incest. Your child may be the person you love the most in the world, but you shouldn't use him as a source of emotional support, at least not very often. While your child is in recovery (or using) you will often need emotional support. You can reach out for support by calling the other parents or your sponsor. If you are feeling overwhelmed or dealing with difficult issues, you may want to make an appointment with the counselor or a therapist.

To care for yourself, you need to set boundaries with regard to your behaviors. For example, you need to set boundaries with regard to how much of your time you give to your job. You are already doing this. But some people set that boundary at the level needed to sustain life—time to eat and sleep and get ready to go to work again. You need to decide for yourself what amount of time to spend at work, and support a meaningful and fulfilling life.

Saying 'No'

You need to set boundaries with regard to how much you do for others. You don't have to take time to drive your young person to every function and take her every place she wants to go at any time. You don't have to say yes to everything your church or the program or the school asks of you. Sometimes, you need to say "no." If you are doing too much, you may have a problem saying no and you need to address it. Some people are afraid that by saying no they will lose a friendship or love. It is your responsibility to manage your life and people will respect you for respecting yourself. Certain people accustomed to you saying yes all the time will be put out at first, but they will get over it.

Most parents of kids in recovery do too much for their kids. Learning when to say no can do a lot to move along the process of recovery. If you have a hard time learning to say no, we recommend that you take responsibility for this issue in a powerful way. There are books on this subject you may want to read. You may want to work a program around it. You may want to accelerate the process by discussing it with the counselor or a therapist. While you are dealing with the issue, listen to the advice of the other parents and your sponsor. They can help you determine when to say no while you are learning to do this for yourself. And remember that when you are confused, when you are asked to give or do something and aren't sure what to do, buy yourself some time. You have a right to take the time you need to decide.

Saying 'Yes' to Good Things

Some parents have boundary problems around not saying yes to good things for themselves. Some parents have such strong boundaries that they won't let anyone else in. For these parents, boundaries are like fortress walls. If you want to do whatever you can to help your child survive this disease, you need the support of the others in the group. You need to let in the love and support of the group.

Trying to Control

Another common boundary issue for parents is control. Parents don't take on being controlling in order to be all-powerful and get their own way. Being controlling is usually a response to experiencing an out-of-control life. It is common for people to be controlling if they were raised in a family where one of the parents was an addict or was abusive. It is a way of surviving emotionally. Parents who are over-controlling of their kids are trying to control their own world and avoid pain and anxiety. It may appear that they are motivated by fear and wanting to protect their child, by love and concern. But underneath is the fear of the feelings they will need to experience if the child doesn't do what they want. Instead of learning to manage their feelings, they try to over-manage what are really outer circumstances. Parents need to identify the feelings that are behind their drive to control and find a healthy way to manage those feelings. They need to let go of the people they are trying to control and learn to support them in effective ways.

Controlling or trying to control another person is a violation of the other person's boundaries and has negative consequences for everyone involved. If you are taking responsibility for controlling your children's feelings, behavior and life, chances are they are not taking responsibility for these things. And they are the only ones with the power to do it. By letting go of control, you will empower your children.

While being over-controlling is common among parents of users, it is a more serious issue in some families than others. Some individual parents may need counseling in order to deal effectively with this issue. Some parents can make a great deal of progress by learning more about the issue and talking to their sponsors. If being over-controlling is an issue for you, addressing this issue presents an opportunity to make a significant contribution to your family's recovery. If you want to do whatever it takes, take this issue on however it applies to you. The result for you will be a giant step toward personal serenity and effectiveness.

Over-Reactive Anger

Over-reactive anger is anger that is in response to more than the incident at hand. It's appropriate to feel anger when our boundaries have been crossed. It's appropriate to express it and, sometimes, to administer consequences. If you feel enraged, however, you are probably experiencing over-reactive anger. This could come from feelings of powerlessness that you haven't accepted. It could be the result of a buildup of negative feelings that you haven't dealt with, stemming from your child's addiction. It could come from your past. If you were abused physically or emotionally as a child, you may react with rage when you can't control your own child.

Some indications of over-reactive anger are frequent physical or verbal abuse, breaking things, or yelling. These behaviors create resentments in the person they are directed at and probably hurt your own self-esteem. They are detrimental to your child's recovery and damage your relationship. Your child must deal with all of the anxieties of growing up and of his own emotional and psychological issues. These anxieties are intensified when they stop using chemicals. His recovery depends on his being able to handle these feelings and issues without turning back to chemicals. Over-reactive anger directed at him will contribute to his resentments and anxieties, adding weight to the wrong side of the scale. You shouldn't try to protect your child from reality—but the more sane you can be during early recovery, the more supportive you will be.

If you experience over-reactive anger, you have a problem and you need to deal with it. You may be able to justify it or rationalize it, but that won't be helpful.

Some parents can deal effectively with their anger by sharing their feelings at meetings and with their sponsor and the other parents. Some will need to deal with boundary issues and control issues. If the over-reactive anger stems from the past, the parent may need personal therapy in order to learn to manage it.

Look over the past month for indications of over-reactive anger and talk to your sponsor about it. If this is an issue for you, come up with a plan to address it.

Meanwhile, when you feel anger, stop, reflect and respond. Call someone. What made you angry? What fears were triggered? What is your best response to the situation at hand?

Make Peace With Your Own Past

Most of us come from weird families. Many of our families were dysfunctional because of chemical abuse. Many of us had a parent (or both parents) who weren't there for us in a healthy way. Some of us experienced some kind of physical or emotional abuse from a member of our family or someone else. Our parents didn't protect us enough, or protected us too much. Any of these things will affect how we feel and behave in our own families today.

Issues coming from these experiences can shape us and run us without our being aware of it. For as long as we are not aware of them, these issues are difficult to deal with. Becoming aware is sometimes all that is needed to manage them.

If you are working a program of recovery, you will eventually do a personal inventory that may uncover an issue from your past. This will be one of the gifts that come from working a program. Once uncovered, you can turn the issue into an opportunity for change and growth. It can provide yet another source of increasing personal serenity and another contribution to the recovery of your young person.

Issues from the past act as blocks to our giving and receiving unconditional love. Unconditional love, and accepting what is at any point in time, are powerful tools for combating this disease. If you can get past your own blocks, and also align yourself with your higher power, you can create miracles.

7

The Choice and the
Consequences

Some young people are attracted into recovery, embrace working a
program and never require intervention from their parents. These kids
have experienced enough and are willing to do whatever it takes to get
sober. Other kids have not experienced enough. They will continue to
relapse until they "hit bottom"—until the pain of continuing to use
outweighs the anticipated pain of getting sober.

Raising Your Child's 'Bottom'

One of the most generous things that parents can do for their young
person is to raise the child's "bottom." This means letting him experience the consequences of his actions such that he will choose to do
whatever it takes to get sober. If we intervene early enough, our children may not have to experience prison or physical deterioration before
they are ready to embrace recovery.

Intervention does not require punishment or kicking kids out of the
house. In fact, parents should not do either of those things. But it may
require that parents demand certain behaviors from their young person
as a condition of living in their home or being supported in other ways.
It is then up to the young person to decide whether he will behave as
required. If he chooses not to live by your principles, he is choosing not
to live in your home. It is important to make it clear to the young person that he is making the choice. He needs to own his decision.

You may have heard kids talk about getting kicked out of their house or parents talk about kicking their kids out. Note how those words take the responsibility off of the user and put it onto the parents. It is crucial for people with this disease to become aware that they are making choices as to how they behave and to own the consequences of their choices. Parents themselves need to clearly understand that they are letting their kids experience the consequences of *the kids' own* choices; the parents are not administering punishment to demonstrate power over their kids. Let the kids be empowered. It's empowering when our actions have effects in the world—even undesirable ones.

Living with another Family in the Program

Not being allowed to live at home does not mean living on the streets. In most cases it means living with another family in the program. The young person will either go to the parent meeting and humbly ask for a place to live temporarily, or talk to individual parents after discussing the situation with the counselor.

The period of time that a child is out of the house will depend on the circumstances. If it is the first time, her or she may only have to leave home for a week. The child will earn his or her way back into the home by working the program to the satisfaction of the parents. The parents may use the counselor for advice on setting the criteria for returning home.

If the child is under 18, the parents may make arrangements with the host family to pay for the child's support. It's best if the parents not provide money directly to the child. The host family can provide the child money for doing chores around the house. If the child is an adult, 18 or older, he should probably earn his or her keep with outside work or by doing work for the host family.

Living with another family serves the young person's recovery in several ways. Most importantly, it lets the child know that her parents mean business. The child is no longer going to be enabled by the parents to continue using or, more importantly, to continue the behaviors which lead to using. When the child realizes this, it may be the turning point to recovery.

Having the young person live in another home also serves to break up the patterns that go on between different people in the family. Young people in their homes are often caught up in rebellious feelings. When they live outside their homes, they are free of those feelings and may find it easier to make positive choices for themselves. If they were used to a lot of care-taking, they get to experience being more independent and taking care of their own needs. If they were accustomed to using a lot of manipulation to get their way with their parents, they will probably find those ways don't work in their new home. The parents, in turn, get to have a break from constant manipulation. They can let go of taking care of their child and let the other family bear the burden of the day-to-day decisions. They gain some distance from their child and develop new, healthier ways to relate to the child and other members of the family.

The host family gets to practice setting and enforcing boundaries with kids who are willing and grateful and with whom they are not overly emotionally attached.

In addition, when the young person comes back home, he has more gratitude, more self-responsibility and less feeling of entitlement.

Choosing to Do It Their Own Way

Sometimes, a young person chooses not to follow the principles for living in the parents' home and is not willing to work a program living in the home of another family in the program. Either the child wants to keep using, or wants to do it his own way. At this juncture, the parents must decide if they want to take a strong stand against the disease or not.

If you are at this decision point, we urge you to think hard before you let the addict set his or her own terms. There are a number of things to consider. How far has the disease progressed? Is the child's life in immediate danger because of the drugs he is using or the people the child is hanging out with? Would you insist on treatment if he had a different disease, such as a brain tumor?

There is a chance that your child can get and stay sober on his own, but there are about the same statistical chances of this happening as an unassisted "miracle" remission from leukemia. Remember: there is no advantage to letting the child have his way with regard to treatment. You are not asking the child to do something horrific. You are telling the child that to live in your home, he must follow a few simple rules that will support his recovery.

If your child isn't willing to live with another family in the program, there are options that would support recovery and provide the child with safety while he is out of your house. The child could enter a lock-in facility for a few months or, perhaps, get admitted to a halfway house for recovering addicts. If the child isn't willing to put himself or into any kind of treatment center, the child can go to a homeless shelter.

If your child won't live by your rules, you will not protect him by letting him stay with you. In fact, he is in more danger being enabled in your home to continue using than if he ran away and had to secure his own food and shelter.

If your child is under-age and does run away instead of accepting any of the choices you have given, you need to call the police and report him as a runaway. If the police find your child and call you, you should do your best not to pick him up until the next day so that the child can have fully experience the consequences. It is a good idea to take a counselor along to get the child. When you pick him up, ask if he is willing to do whatever it takes to get sober. Also, offer him the same choices you offered before. If the child chooses one, good. If he chooses not to take one, and if he would rather run away than live by your rules, call the police and turn the child in as a runaway again.

If your child runs away, it is most probable that the police won't be calling—your child will. Most kids will want desperately to get back into their homes within a few days. First they will go from friend to friend and sleep on their couches. It might be exciting at first. But it gets old fast. They don't have their own space. They have no certainty of food and shelter. Their friends get sick of them. They are scared. And they miss their parents.

You will want to make a plan with the counselor as to what to do when your child calls and wants to come home. You may want to have your child call the counselor and work out the terms with him.

While your child is out as a runaway, you will experience a lot of anxiety and sadness. You may want to hunt him down and try to talk him into coming back home—but that won't accomplish anything. During this time you need to take care of yourself and your anxious feelings. You may need to go to meetings every day. You will need to talk to people every day. You will probably be consumed with doubts. "What if he gets assaulted? What if he gives up?" You need to hang on to knowing that you are doing the right thing. Your son or daughter is in more danger by your enabling him or her to use than when the child is out on his own. And while your child is out, his options are still in front of him. He can come back any time he is ready to do what it takes to treat the disease that is killing him.

From one mother in the group:

Our son Mike was a very hard case, and so were we. We stayed in denial for months in the face of the most obvious evidence of drug use. For example, we drug-tested him about every two weeks, and he failed every time. I think we believed his explanations of this phenomenon because we didn't know what to do. We didn't come out of denial until he made a fairly serious suicide attempt.

He found the program through a friend at school and got sober and then relapsed while in the program. We were told by the counselor that he was relapsing, but we didn't believe it. We went on enabling him by letting him live at home until he overdosed and ended up at the hospital in intensive care.

Twice during his recovery, we had to give him a choice of living with another family or going to a residential treatment center. Both times he was underage and ran away from home instead. He was out living various places for five weeks the first time and four months the second time. While he was, out he had many unpleasant experiences but, fortunately, none of them were life-threatening. While being enabled at home, he almost died twice.

We can't tell you that your child will not be at risk if he is out on his own without resources, but we can tell you unequivocally that he is at great risk when living in your home and not treating his disease. Also, be assured that your young person wants to live and to be comfortable even more than you want it for him. If he is choosing to be out of the house and in danger, he is very sick with this disease and is not safe being enabled to remain in it.

Help from Police, Child Protective Services, the Judicial System and County Health Services

You may not get support from government agencies that you expect. The police can be very understanding of parents who are trying to take a stand with their kids and can, to an extent, cooperate with parents. In some cases you can help them help you by doing things your way. For example, if the police call for you to come and pick up your child, call the counselor before you go. It may be better to leave him in overnight. The police won't want to keep him but if you don't pick him up, they will.

The judicial system is changing with regard to juvenile crime. If your child has to go to court, discuss it with the counselor. You may or may not be advised to support your child's defense if she has committed a crime. You will have to decide if the range of likely sentences from the court would help or hurt your child's recovery. If she is underage and caught with drugs, you may want the judicial system to back you up by sentencing your child to a short stay in juvenile detention or some serious probation with a strong stipulation to be involved in accountable treatment. Sometimes a judge will give an offender the choice of prison or treatment. That could provide the right opportunity for your child to choose treatment.

Child Protective Services will not help you with your own children if you are trying to get them into treatment. At least in Texas, Child Protective Services (CPS) doesn't have anything to offer you. If you don't let your child live in your home without providing him an alternative, and if you have not turned her in as a runaway, then CPS can take you, the parents, to court and attempt to terminate your parental rights. However, if you have grandchildren, CPS may be helpful in finding a temporary foster home for the children if their parents are unfit to care for them.

County health services may provide free or low-cost residential treatment for addicts. What is difficult, but not impossible, is getting your child committed to a lock-in facility against his will. In Harris County, Texas, if you get a warrant for your child's arrest on the basis that she is suicidal or homicidal, the county will keep your child for three days. After that, if she is not found to be suicidal or homicidal, she will be allowed to leave.

The bottom line is that there is little governmental or societal support for parents who take a stand against the disease. Parents need to be aware of the opportunities and dangers that their public services present and work them to their advantage as best they can. It is advisable to seek consultation from a counselor to negotiate this minefield of intervention.

If You Must Do It, Do It Well

When there is a difficult task to do, there is always a way to do it better. Because you may torment yourself with how you handle this task, we recommend that you do it as well as you can. It may make some difference to your child and the outcome. It will definitely make a difference in how you feel while your child is out of your house. Please don't use these thoughts to beat yourself up afterwards. You are not going to do it perfectly, and it is not going to make much difference how you do it. This is for *you*, not them.

First, tell your child that he has not been living by the principles you established for living in your home. Remind him that he knew that living by these rules was a condition for living at home. Then you can remind him about what his remaining options are. If he doesn't like them, he will have to find his own way. You may want to give him some change and a copy of the phone lists: the parent list and the group list.

You will be most effective if you do this without anger and without tears. Do it without anger because it is not a punishment, it is the reality of the consequences of his choice. Do it without tears because you do not want to give the impression that it hurts you more than it does him, or that it is tragic. He is simply going to stay in another home for awhile.

And do it with love. Tell him how much you love him and that it is because you love him that you are willing to take this stand against the disease.

While he is living outside of your house, don't be his caretaker. Let your child take care of himself. This will give him self-esteem—which he needs to get well. Instead, turn your care-taking needs onto yourself so that you can maintain your strength and clarity of mind. Go to lots of meetings and talk to lots of parents. Call the counselor and find out how things are going.

If your child chooses to run away, all of the advice above applies to you. But you will need additional support and you should ask for it.

Spend time developing your conscious contact with your higher power. You may, during this time, receive spiritual gifts you didn't expect. Take comfort in the serenity prayer. In very painful times, you may want to repeat it over and over to yourself.

Practice living in the present. Focus on the way the bed sheet feels against your skin. Focus on the sounds of your house. Remind yourself that you are OK right now. At this moment, everything really *is* OK. Remember, your young person is either feeling OK right now or moving toward coming back home. So right now, at this moment, he is OK, too. If you learn to be in the present (and this time may be the first time you are really able to do this), and if you let yourself be supported by the group, your experience while your child is out may be surprisingly rewarding.

Dealing with Unwanted Enablers

If your child runs away from home, he may find himself under the care of an unwary enabler. Perhaps the parents of one of your child's friends who uses drugs will take your child in. The parents will have their own reasons for doing so. If the people don't try to contact you or call the police, they may be acting out a rescuing fantasy or having their own needs met in some way by taking care of your child.

You should talk to these people and let them know what is going on and the options that your child has. It is unlikely, however, that they will understand. After all, if they can see that you are doing the right thing in taking a stand against the disease, then what are *they* doing? Ask them not to let your child stay with them any longer. Let them know that they are harboring a runaway and that you will report them to the police if they persist. If they still don't cooperate, you need to turn them in to the police.

If your child is 17 or older, he is of age to leave home, and so it is not clear that the enabling person is breaking the law. They are, however, interfering with the treatment of your child's disease and you might be able to hold them liable for that. What you need to do in this situation is to make the enablers very uncomfortable. You need to give them anxiety so that they will find a reason to make your child leave their home. Let them know the situation and that they are enabling your child to continue using drugs and that they are interfering with your child's treatment. Send them a registered letter with this information and let them know that you hold them responsible for the results of their interference. Send them a follow-up letter threatening to take civil action against them for interfering with your child's treatment. Or have a lawyer write the letter. Even if the enablers believe that you won't win such a lawsuit, the thought of being taken to court on these kinds of charges should give them so much anxiety that they will want your child to leave.

Parents of your child's friends aren't the only enablers. The enabler may be an employer, your child's friend or lover, or a relative. Given enough time, the enabler will probably get tired of your child. You will need to decide if there is time to let the situation play out on its own or if you need to intervene. If it is time to intervene, you will be able to find a way to make the person uncomfortable.

Back in Recovery

When your young person returns home, or embraces recovery, it will be a time for inward rejoicing. Your son or daughter is out of danger for the moment and on the path to health and sobriety. You may have experienced the last relapse.

Enjoy the moment fully—you deserve it. But don't let yourself be wooed back into denial. Coming off of relapse, your young person has re-entered early sobriety. Her brain will be calling her back to chemical highs and she probably has strengthened friendships with people who want her to use drugs. Her brain chemistry has been recently damaged and it will take time to heal. How well you support her by setting and enforcing boundaries, modeling recovery behaviors and accepting her as she is today will make a difference on whether she continues growing in recovery, or relapses again.

If your son has come back to you embracing sobriety, you should both rejoice and get ready. This is not an end, or a beginning.

It is progress.

8

Choosing Faith and Using the Power of Acceptance

"Prayer is not an old woman's amusement. Properly understood and applied, it is the most potent instrument of action."

—Mohandas K. Gandhi

Effectively parenting a young person through addiction may, at times, entail taking positions that require superhuman strength. It is likely that you will be called upon to take actions that are counterintuitive, that go against everything you have previously learned to do as a parent, and for which you will get little or no support from people who are not in some kind of recovery program themselves.

To be able to take the actions needed for your child to survive this disease, you need to develop your own spirituality. Note that we do not say that you need to become religious. Nor is there a particular belief system that is required. Developing conscious contact with your higher power is required.

With the help of God, you can get your son or daughter back. By choosing to have faith in a higher power, you become able to let go and "let God," and get out of the way of recovery. It is by choosing faith that you can take a stand against the disease and not "rescue" your young person from suffering the consequences of her choices. Without choosing faith, fear will stop you. What is simple will appear complex and confusing. And what is easy will seem to be impossible.

More importantly, your growing spirituality will open the door for miracles. Much can be accomplished by parents doing the right things and taking the right stands. But there is a higher level of effectiveness that a parent can access where the effects are immediate and perfect.

The Power of Acceptance

Acceptance is probably the most powerful principle to be mastered.

It seems like acceptance would hold no power. It even sounds almost cowardly at first, like a resting place for failures. But the quiet peace of acceptance actually is a powerful force that produces unexpected results in our world.

To create healing in ourselves and others, we must start with accepting what is. Acceptance of the way things are makes possible creating something different. You have probably read this before, or experienced it in your own life. To not accept the way things are as the truth about the way things are is what we call "denial."

To explore this further, let's begin with self-acceptance. Psychologists know that self-acceptance is necessary before change can occur in an individual. Self-acceptance is not self-esteem. Self-acceptance can be attained in an instant. Self-esteem is earned over time. If a person has attained self-acceptance, he or she can begin to build self-esteem.

Self-acceptance does not mean that you approve of all aspects of yourself, or that there are not things about yourself that you wish to change or improve. It means that you do not deny what is true for you right now. You may think that you are overweight and want to lose pounds. If you can accept that you are overweight right now, and not be at war with that fact, then you have self-acceptance and are in a place where change is possible. On the other hand, if you cannot allow yourself to be fully aware of your current state, you are in a state of denial and cannot make conscious rational decisions about that aspect of your life.

Once you attain self-acceptance, it is easy to make the decisions and take the actions that lead to attaining self-esteem.

Many people have experienced the peace and freedom that come about when self-acceptance has been attained after a period of non-self-acceptance. If you have experienced this, then you know how issues that once seemed insurmountable and changes that seemed unattainable can become almost effortless.

This power that comes with self-acceptance also shows up, though not necessarily instantaneously, when we accept things outside of ourselves.

Unconditional love is the acceptance of ourselves or others exactly as they are at this moment in time. When unconditional love is present, it is heard or felt by the person who is receiving it, and it is healing for them. It seems that when we can give another person our unconditional love and acceptance, it opens the way for that person to love and accept himself unconditionally. It's as though we are holding up a mirror for him that reflects the perfection of his inner being, allowing him to see this for himself. And when he gets that self-acceptance, things he had been resisting about himself lose some of their power.

The following is the experience of one mother in the parent group:

"For several years we had struggled with our older daughter, who had obsessive-compulsive disorder. Our other daughter, Vanessa, was perfect. She was always pleasant and never gave us any trouble. Looking back, I believe Vanessa put up a front of pleasantness and behaved perfectly because she didn't think our family could manage any more trouble. She was probably right. The illness of our older daughter, our fears for our older daughter, and the daily stress of living with a child with obsessive-compulsive disorder kept us in a state of extreme stress and despair.

"Later, when she was in the fifth grade, Vanessa also started showing disturbing symptoms. I don't know what pushed her over the edge. It could have been the stress of holding in all her own thoughts and fears for so long. It might have been compounded by academic stress. In any case, one day she started holding her hands in fists—all the time. And she started twitching. When she looked at me, she would sort of blink one eye and twist her

head down. She did this about every 10 seconds. I hated this twitching most of all. It made her look mentally ill and it tormented me.

"We took Vanessa to a psychiatrist believing that she, like her sister, had obsessive-compulsive disorder (OCD). She was not diagnosed that way. The psychiatrist recommended family counseling. But I was certain that Vanessa had the problem and that our family was fine, and we did not go into family counseling. (We were wrong, of course.)

"One day, after two months of Vanessa's twitching, I left our house in despair and went for a walk. I was certain that Vanessa could have been fine but that the stress in our house had finally been too much for her. But how could I get rid of the stress? Our other daughter kept us on edge with her OCD symptoms, and how could we stop worrying when these problems were real? Then I got it. I would give my daughters what they needed and accept them exactly as they are—even if they are mentally ill. It was so clear at that moment. And it gave me peace. I walked back to the house.

"As I approached the house, I wondered how long I could hold on to this new insight and this new peace. I walked up the sidewalk and Vanessa met me halfway. I looked at her and she did the twitch thing. I didn't say anything to her but I thought at her. I thought at her for the purpose of keeping my own thoughts straight. I thought, 'Go ahead Vanessa and twitch. Twitch all you want, because we are going to be a fun family that twitches and makes fists and does all kinds of weird things, but we'll have fun.' I thought that at her and I walked on into the house.

"The interesting thing is that she never did it again. She had done that twitch thing every 10 seconds or so for two months, and I never saw her do it again.

"I believe two things because of this experience. I believe that we hear each other on an unconscious level—at least we hear some things. And I am convinced that what Vanessa heard, the thing that made the difference, is that in that one moment, I accepted her as she was—with the twitch. The twitch was not an issue any more."

To unconditionally love our children, we need to accept them with all of their weaknesses, addictions and problems. The mother in the story above did not accept her daughter in spite of the twitch. She loved and accepted her, twitch and all.

We need to accept that our substance-abusing young people are substance abusers. This means that we love them and accept them even when they are substance abusers. This means not resisting but acknowledging what is true about them at this time. It's not what we had hoped for or expected or what we want in the future, but this is what is so for them today. And at this moment in time, we love them with the disease. At this moment, we can accept that this is true for them at this time.

So how do we develop this acceptance, this unconditional love? We come back to the need to develop our spirituality, our conscious contact with our higher power. Is unconditional love and acceptance not what we seek to develop, as taught by all of our world's major religions? For those who choose to practice these ideals, they are a lifelong pursuit, but ones of which we can enjoy immediate success *one moment at a time*.

We can demonstrate unconditional love and acceptance of our children by giving them our time and attention, by listening to them without judging, and by enjoying their company. This can be simple: a little time, a little listening without judging, and letting yourself enjoy your child for a few minutes without trying to fix anything. At least it will be simple if you make that your goal for a given opportunity.

Here are a few tips that may help:

- Make a conscious decision regarding a particular time you will be spending together, and how you will behave during that time, and keep it simple. "My goal is to listen without judging tonight." "My goal is to enjoy my daughter just as she is tonight and not look for ways to fix her."

- Plan to take a few minutes just before your time together, to pray and to bring back your awareness of acceptance and unconditional love.

- Decide in advance that if fears and concerns or "good advice" come into your head during your time together, you will set them aside and think about them later.

- Target a time that will be short. Five perfect minutes could be just the thing to start with.

- Be prepared with some thought or phrase to keep yourself focused on loving unconditionally. This thought could be an articulation of your goal. It could be a repetition of your acceptance as thoughts come to your consciousness: "I accept that you don't look me in the eye tonight." "I accept that you choose to decorate yourself this way tonight." "I accept that we are going through all of this craziness together." "I accept our lives aren't the way I had planned." Or this thought could be an expression that gives you a sense of peace: "This is a beautiful child of God." "God is in charge." "For 15 minutes I can let myself enjoy the beauty of my son's face."

You can take this one step further by listening to what you have been unwilling to hear in the past. This could be your child's view on some issue that you think is ridiculous and don't even want to hear. It could be complaints about you or your spouse or your church. If you really listen, your young person will feel heard and valued. Also, it could take some of the power out of his opinion, complaint or stand.

There are a couple of ways to set this up. If you know what the issue is, you can just ask them to share it with you. Let them know that while you have not been willing to listen to it in the past, now you are. If you don't know of a particular issue that you wouldn't listen to in the past, you can ask. "Is there anything that you've been telling me but I haven't heard you because I wouldn't listen? Because I want to listen now."

Arranging a time to be with your young person may itself be a challenge. If your son or daughter doesn't drive yet, you might take advantage of a car ride. The car provides a chance for conversation without discomfort. Having one of you with your eyes on the road and occupied with driving diffuses the intensity. There's a reason for you to remain in close proximity for a little while. And silences in the car are not uncomfortable. If you set yourself up to be an accepting listener in the car, your teenager probably will talk.

Another possibility is taking your young person out to eat. At a restaurant there is time and an alternative focus—food.

If you don't feel ready for any of this, there is another approach that is equally powerful. You can do this without your child being physically present. If it is your daughter's life that you are upset about, sit comfortably by yourself and contemplate the miracle that is your daughter. First, focus on the wonderful, loving person you know she really is. Then, focus on the ways she is that you don't like and be aware of your love for her. Remember that it is not that you don't want things to change. It is that you can accept for right now things exactly as they are. "My daughter could be putting chemicals in her body right now. It's not what I want, but at this moment I can accept that this is true and I am loving her even as she is right now. My love for her is real." "My daughter has a shaved head and at this moment I can accept that this is how she is choosing to look for now, and I love her." Try to bring a moment's focus to the things that you dislike the most: the body piercings, the jarring hairstyle, the attitude, the low self-esteem. By accepting for a moment the truth about the way things are, you may allow those things to disappear.

9

Moving On

Recovery is forever, but participation in an early recovery program has a beginning, middle and end.

Early recovery in an alternative, peer-group program is a unique time when your family is part of a community of parents and young people committed to supporting each other. It is an amazing time of extreme fear and sadness, miracles, mutual love and support, and celebration of life.

During the first several months, the counselor may encourage the young person to focus only on getting sober and getting connected with the group members who can teach him how.

Once the young person has embraced the principles of recovery and established some sobriety, he enters into what we call second-stage recovery. During this stage, he continues practicing the principles of recovery and applies them to all areas of his life. He develops his relationship with a higher power. He learns to do what he has committed to do, rather than what might feel good at the time. He learns to set healthy boundaries and manage his emotions in a constructive way. He focuses on being responsible to himself and others in relationships and at work or school. Unless the user learns to be responsible and successful in these important aspects of life, and not let the disease sabotage him, he will not be able to maintain sobriety.

A young person must show he is able to manage himself in these areas critical to sobriety before the counselor will tell him that it is time to leave the program and move on to a permanent program such as Alcoholics Anonymous, which is not counselor-directed.

To demonstrate that he is ready to move on to the new program, the young person has other people in his life attest to his readiness. He will have his sponsor attest that the young person is engaged with the program. His program sponsor will attest that he has a working knowledge of the Twelve Steps and worked the first five to the sponsor's satisfaction. The young person's parents will attest that he has a working relationship with his family. He will show he has had six months of success at full-time work, school, or a combination of the two.

Moving on is taken very seriously and is celebrated. The young person will probably have a good-bye meeting and participate in a commemoration of "awakening." After that, he will no longer regularly attend meetings of the early-recovery group.

Parents need to continue to participate in the early-recovery program for as long as their young person is participating. And while their young person is working on second-stage recovery, the parents need to be as committed to maintaining boundaries and requiring certain behaviors as when the young person was just getting sober. In fact, the parents must forever be on guard to being used by the disease and relapsing into enabling or codependent behaviors.

If the parents protect their young person from the consequences of irresponsible behavior, the young person may not have sufficient motivation to succeed at work, school and relationships. And again, if the young person does not establish success in these areas—he likely will relapse.

And just as most addicts need to continue attending recovery meetings on a regular ongoing basis, parents also need continued support to avoid a relapse. They are encouraged to attend meetings of Codependents Anonymous (CODA), Al-Anon or another recovery group. This way, the parents will continue to grow, be more vigilant to the signs of relapse in their young person and have the support they need if the young person does relapse.

Moving on is necessary to a healthy life. The counselor/client relationship must end and be replaced by a friendship of equals. The closed community of people committed to recovery must be replaced by other communities, some committed to recovery, some unrelated.

When an individual is ready to move on, he usually wants to. He takes with him the disease and the potential for relapse. He also takes what he has learned in recovery and a commitment to leading a healthy life.

As a final word, there is a great deal about this disease we still don't know. We do know it is complicated. We do know it is confusing. We do know it is devastating to its victims and their loved ones. We don't know a quick, surefire, cookie-cutter approach that "cures" everyone. Rightfully, the disease has traditionally been characterized with the adjectives, "cunning," "baffling" and "powerful."

The good news is that it is virtually absolute that should a sufferer or loved one practice the principles and procedures we have talked about in this book, recovery is not only attainable—but probable.

PART II

Questions and Answers

"Life is like playing a violin solo in public and learning the instrument as one goes on."

—Samuel Butler

This part addresses issues that come up while parenting a young person in early recovery. They are presented in question-and-answer format. Our hope is that the answers will provide you more background as you address these issues in your own family, but we advise you not to apply these suggestions directly to your own situation without discussing it with a program counselor.

Each family's situation is different, and nuances can prove critically significant. What is effective in the first few weeks of recovery may not be effective two months later. What will work in one family's situation may not work in another's. The program counselor can advise you based on the particular circumstances of your child's case.

1. **How can I tell if my daughter really needs to be in the program? She told me that she doesn't have a problem with drugs, that she only tried marijuana a couple times. I don't want to expose my child to kids who have serious problems, if my child has only experimented.**

    First, eliminate the notion of "experimentation" with drugs. Our kids are not conducting experiments. This term has been grabbed hold of by parents, kids and our culture to stay in denial. Our culture talks about the importance of prevention and early intervention, but when faced with the early signs of drug or alcohol use, those of us affected want to minimize or not even acknowledge the situation, oftentimes hiding behind the smokescreen of "experimentation."

    When we are confronted with "experimentation," we should respond with intervention—swift and sure. Remember that drugs can be defined as poison ingested by various means in (hopefully) non-lethal amounts, but in amounts that are mentally, emotionally, physically, spiritually, and developmentally debilitating.

Even if your child really has only used one or two times, you should intervene. It is not a small thing to be putting these chemicals into his body; it causes physiological changes in the brain. Smoking a little marijuana is a very big concern. This does not mean, however, that your child should necessarily enter a recovery program. Program counselors are trained and able to determine whether the young person needs the program. The key is whether the young person has bought into the "outlaw mindset" that was discussed in Chapter Four. The counselor will be able to determine this in the assessment process. Parents usually are not in a position to determine this. Self-diagnosis of chemical dependency is as dangerous as self-diagnosis of leukemia, diabetes, tuberculosis or any other chronic, progressive, fatal disease. Parents need an expert opinion.

The likelihood is, however, that if your child is admitting to using one or two times, she has actually used a whole lot more. Children often have admitted to using one or two times because that's how many times they were caught. Or they are playing a rendition of the manipulative game of Tell a Little Truth to Cover a Big Lie. Some kids who have not been caught yet but are regularly using will claim they have tried drugs and didn't like them, to throw their parents off the path. Realize that it is rare for kids who have tried drugs and not liked them to admit this to their parents, if they don't have to. And it is rare for kids when they first come into the recovery program to admit to their parents the full extent of their use.

As for being concerned about your child entering a recovery program because it places him around kids who have used drugs—if your child has used, then he is already hanging around with kids who use. In fact, in most cases today, if your child is in school, going to church or in organized sports—unless he is a hermit or complete recluse—he is around drugs. In the program, he will hang around with kids who have used drugs but have decided they don't want to any more and are succeeding in their efforts.

Our estimate is that at any one time, about 85 percent of kids in an established alternative peer group (APG) are succeeding at living out their commitment to responsible living, free of mind-changing chemicals. Kids in the program—at least most of them—have made that decision and are learning to do what it takes to get and stay sober. They will not only provide the best possible peer group for your child to get sober in, but you cannot help your child get and stay sober without them.

Other behaviors are warning signs of a substance-abuse problem. For many kids, *but not all,* grades will suddenly drop. Users change their friends. They stop caring about things they used to. They avoid real communication with parents. They are angry with their parents for no apparent reason. They lie about where they are going and whom they are with.

If you know that the kids your child is hanging out with are users, even periodically, it is almost certain your child is using, too, or is in the process of drifting toward usage. Kids who use generally don't like hanging out with kids who don't. And likewise, kids who don't use generally don't enjoy hanging out with kids who do. This tends to be true of adults, as well. There are a few exceptions, but the exceptions are rare.

2. **How can I get my daughter into the program if she doesn't want to go?**

Program counselors are trained in intake and intervention. They are the experts at getting young people into treatment. If you listen to the counselors and work with them, it probably will be easy to get your daughter to make a 30-day commitment to the program.

Your working with the counselor is what will make it easy. Usually, if the parent is willing to give support, the counselor can get a young person to choose to come into the program. The addict also will agree to do the following three things for 30 days: come to two meetings per week; make the kids in the program their friends (and give up their old friends); and stay sober. The kids will promise those three things because they think they can con adults on two of them: staying sober, and giving up their old friends. For those first 30 days, the kids probably won't give up their friends or stay sober. But we have got what we really want—we have them in meetings for a month, where they will start socializing with kids in recovery and start learning the tools they need to get sober.

Sometimes this doesn't work. Sometimes parents have to square off with their young person to get her to come into the program. They may have to take a stand and say, "We love you too much to sit by and watch you kill yourself. You have to start going to meetings and work on getting sober. This is the house rule, and if you aren't willing to follow it, then we will have to do something more serious."

3. **Should I let my child go to coffee after the meetings on school nights?**

Coffee is an informal gathering after a program, often meeting at a coffee shop, restaurant or member's home. Most nights, there is a mix of lighthearted fun and serious personal sharing. The most important factor for kids to get into early recovery is a connection with the other kids in recovery, and coffee is where a lot of that connection gets made.

Whether your child should go to coffee on school nights depends on a variety of factors, so you should discuss this with the counselor. If you have a young person tied into the kids at school or in the neighborhood, and he is not tied in with the kids in the program, it is probably best if you let him go to coffee on school nights. If the counselor agrees, it might be best to allow some prioritization of your young person getting to know the other kids, even if it might hurt his school performance. Staying out until 2 a.m. probably is not the best thing. But this also depends on your young person's situation.

If your child is tied in with the family, his acting out has been minimal, he is anxious to establish sobriety, is saddened that he has this disease and is willing to follow the process of recovery, then prioritize some time for him to get tied in with the other kids in recovery. But set some reasonable boundaries, too.

On the other hand, if your child ran away from home for two months to Los Angeles and has been pimping or prostituting or carrying a gun, putting a 10:30 p.m. curfew on him is not going to work. Consult with the counselor about what will be most effective for your child.

4. **My husband and I are social drinkers. Do we need to stop having alcohol in the house?**

    We strongly recommend that you create an alcohol-free, drug-free home. Also, while your young person is in early recovery, we request that you not drink even outside the home.

    Parents' behavior does affect the child's behavior. If you are saying don't use and you are using, then your behavior is saying it's OK to use. And if there is alcohol kept in your home, you are providing a source of temptation that a teenager in early recovery doesn't need. If your child had diabetes, was unstable in treating it and craved sweets, how many sweets would you eat in front of him and how many chocolate cakes would you keep in your home? It's the same thing with substance abuse. It, too, is a disease.

    Your child may tell you that seeing you drink doesn't have any effect on him. You should not take statements like that as a true reading of the effects of your drinking or the presence of alcohol in your home.

If you find yourself or your spouse resisting giving up alcohol while your child is in treatment, then be aware of that. It might be an indication that one of you is chemically dependent. It might be that you or your spouse has an allegiance to using alcohol and is giving it a priority that is inappropriate when you have a child fighting this disease. Or it could mean that one of you does not understand the seriousness of the disease, and therefore is not prepared to take uncomfortable steps needed to combat the disease.

5. **Should I enforce a curfew?**

There are two types of curfews: the one you adopt for your family, and legal curfews. We recommend that you at least adopt the legal curfew of the city or county you live in and the jurisdictions that your son or daughter may be in on a particular night. Living inside the law is a reasonable boundary to set. The alternative is condoning breaking the law, which contradicts taking a stand for living a responsible, principle-based life.

There may be some kids who come into the program for whom putting a high priority on curfew would not be effective early in recovery. These are kids who did a lot of acting out before they came into the program. Therefore, we recommend that you discuss this with the program counselor.

In any case, if your child is arrested for breaking curfew, do not come to her rescue. Let her suffer the consequences of her decisions that the judicial system provides.

6. **Should I give up on what my child looks like and what his bedroom looks like?**

With regard to kids' bedrooms, that is their place. We want them to feel comfortable at home. And we want them to have a place they can go to be alone. If they are staying sober and trying to establish a relationship with God, then a couple of peanut butter sandwiches under the bed attracting roaches is probably not very important.

As parents, when the big issues start to get under control, we tend to turn our attention to lesser issues. When we do that, we often focus our anxiety and anger on these secondary issues. Pushing on these secondary issues will irritate your child and probably cause resentment. While there are limits to what is reasonable to tolerate, it's best if you can let that room be his.

One issue we have to consider regarding dress is respect. There are times we dress a certain way to show respect. When this co-author goes to a funeral, I wear a suit. If I attend a play my children are in, I don't wear the same clothes I just wore to mow the lawn. I dress in a way that won't cause them any discomfort. Physical appearance in public places carries an element of mutual respect, and it is appropriate for us to teach this to our children. But when it comes to how our kids look when they are just hanging out with each other, we should back off and leave that to them.

An aspect of dress is its communicative side. Kids need to become aware of what they are communicating by how they dress and decorate themselves. They need to become aware of what actually is being communicated to not only their peers, but others. For example, a young girl may be dressing to say that she is maturing sexually into a woman. She needs to learn that older men may interpret her dress as indicating she is sexually available. A boy may be wearing a T-shirt with symbols of violence to show his affiliation with a particular group of kids who like a particular kind of music, and to show that he is tough. Adults may perceive him as dangerous.

Kids need a chance to learn that they are in relation to others with how they dress. They don't live in a vacuum. What they wear is *not* just about them. They are sending messages, and these messages are being interpreted differently by different people. Kids will learn this best from the kids in the recovery group and the counselor.

Parents should not try to control how their young people dress, but may need to set a limit depending on the occasion or because of excessive inappropriateness. But parents should avoid playing out their own prejudices on their teenagers with regard to dress. And they need to pick their battles.

7. **Can my daughter get sober in the next three months before school starts? I'm worried about her grades.**

Every case is different. It is possible for your daughter to get sober in three months and stay sober for the rest her life. But the early-recovery process takes longer than three months. Generally, it takes 18 months to three years to stabilize and be ready to move on to a non-staffed program, such as Alcoholics Anonymous.

During the first months of recovery, sobriety needs to be the No. 1 priority for most kids. During this time, school performance may improve due to sobriety, or worsen. Some kids are careful to keep school on track while they are using drugs, to keep their parents from suspecting what they doing. Once their drug use is known, kids let their school performance drop. In some cases, school performance drops after recovery has begun due to eliminating chemical crutches such as amphetamines, or the reinstitution of a sense of guilt about cheating. Also, there is a reemergence of feelings in early sobriety which demand time and attention and detract from the ability to focus on schoolwork.

It will help if the parents can let go of school performance for awhile. This is very hard for parents, especially if the young person has not acted out very much with the disease. When the young person's life is obviously at risk, it is easier. School means nothing if the child is not going to survive. But as soon as the young person gets sober, old parental expectations reassert themselves. Old hopes, dreams and expectations for our kids rush back in—sometimes too soon.

Recovery takes time. After your child has put some time together sober, has learned the basic principles of recovery and incorporated those principles into everyday life, then it will be time to move into what we call second-stage recovery. In second-stage recovery, there is a focus on, among other things, school and work. It is essential to long-term recovery to be able to succeed and be responsible with regard to school and work. In fact, in order for the counselor to recommend discharge from the program, the young person must demonstrate success at meeting the requirements of full-time school, full-time work or a combination of the two.

8. **I get confused when my child is pressuring me for money, or permission to do something, or for me to do some service for them. What can I do?**

Buy yourself time. Tell her that you need some time to think about it, and insist on that right. You do not have to give an answer immediately. Your child can wait a few minutes or even longer, and her ride can wait, or she can miss whatever it is she is pressuring you about. If you feel even a little confused, say, "Stop. I need to talk to my sponsor about this before I give you an answer. If you need an answer immediately, the answer is no." Then pray about it, call your sponsor or another parent, and talk it through until you are ready to make a decision.

Afterwards, forgive yourself quickly if you think you made the wrong decision.

9. **I think my child is suicidal. Can I trust that the group will give him the support he needs?**

If your child is talking about suicide or homicide, take it seriously. Put him in the hospital. If you think he might be just talking suicide or homicide for attention or for manipulative reasons, let him learn that when he say things like that, he gets put in the hospital.

You also should call the program counselors and enlist their help. This situation needs more attention than the group and group meetings will provide.

10. **Should I spy on my kids to make sure they are sticking with winners?**

No, but you should stay aware. If you think they are hanging out with the wrong kids, call and let the counselor know, and the counselor will confront them if it's appropriate. The kids in the program who have bought into recovery will also be letting the counselor know. Breaking the secrecy around the disease goes a long way towards breaking the disease.

11. **Should I have my child take a drug test?**

If you have a reason to do a drug test, you should. And it doesn't hurt to do it periodically. But you should be careful about how you use the results.

In the first weeks of recovery, it is common for kids to relapse even though they are starting to make progress with regard to doing the things they need to in order to get and stay sober. Also, they may pass a drug test, even though they are not doing the things they must to maintain sobriety. Recovery in this program centers around detection of the behaviors that lead to relapse, *not* the detection of relapse.

Also, drug tests are not necessarily reliable. The kids can buy herbal products at stores that mask illicit substances and enable them to pass a urinalysis even if they are using.

12. **My husband/wife won't come to meetings. Should I keep the pressure on?**

There are a number of reasons why some parents won't come to meetings. And there are a number of different ways to intervene when one parent is not participating. You should consult with the counselor and other parents in the program about your particular situation.

You should keep coming to meetings yourself whether or not your spouse or the child's other parent comes. If he won't come to meetings, maybe he will agree to read this book and to meet with counselors from time to time.

The non-participating parent may not understand the nature of the disease and the importance of parental involvement. In that case, continuing to feed him information may eventually make the difference.

Some parents don't get involved because they are afraid. These parents may come in when they start to get some hope that their child can come through this.

Some parents don't come in because they themselves have a problem with chemical addiction that they don't want to confront. There may need to be an intervention with the parent concerning his own addiction.

The support of all parents is important enough that we recommend that you maintain an effective and compassionate stand for their participation. "Effective and compassionate" are important qualifiers. We think you should use all of your tact and all of what you know about the other person to help him understand the disease and the need for his help.

If you want to do everything you can to support your child's recovery, then you may want to focus some of your effort toward improving your relationship with your spouse or the other parent.

It is possible that there is something going on in your relationship that is stopping the other's participation in the program. This same issue may be an issue with your child. If you improve your relationship with the other adult, it may have a significant effect on your child's recovery. And it only takes one parent—you—to start making positive changes.

13. **I think my son might still be using. Should I let him drive the car?**

No. If your son is using, his chances of getting in a car accident are pretty high. This means that his life, the lives of his friends and the lives of other people are at risk. If he were in an accident with injuries you would be morally, if not legally, at fault. That would be hard for you and your son to live with.

If you don't trust your son, it is because of his behavior. You do not have to apologize for not trusting him. And giving him the benefit of the doubt does not serve anyone. Letting him experience the natural consequences of his behavior—in this case, not trusting him—will serve him well. Passively waiting for a serious accident to serve as a natural consequence would be irresponsible, and possibly tragic.

14. **Is this program a cult?**

No. For one thing, we do everything we can to get young people and their parents to leave the program. Cults want you for a lifetime. We serve families during early recovery, generally for a period that lasts from 18 months to three years. Once the young person has met the criteria for being awakened (our word for discharged), it is time for her to move on to another program, such as AA. We take discharge very seriously. Everything in the program is aimed at getting your child to not need the program any more.

The charge of cult usually comes from the kids or codependent parents. At some point, your young person may get uncomfortable in the program and want out. This may happen because she is being held accountable or doesn't want to face some using issue with the group. Or she may be frustrated by her inability to manipulate you, and want to discredit the program. At these times, she may tell you that the program is a cult and that you are being brainwashed.

New parents may wonder if the program is a cult because the kids in early recovery are supposed to hang out only with "winners"—winners being defined as kids committed to recovery, who will hold them accountable and, in most cases, are in the program. Sticking with winners is key to young people getting sober, and it is the cornerstone of the program. It is also a key principle of AA, where the slogan "Stick with winners" originated. Over time, recovering addicts can broaden their circle of friends to include people outside of recovery. But in early recovery, young people cannot.

Sometimes, parents wonder if the program is a cult, because they hear things they don't want to hear. We do not offer comfort for someone who wants to pretend everything is OK or is going to be OK without doing anything about it.

Another red flag for you as a parent is that you are asked to trust the program, the counselors and the process. And you are asked to not necessarily trust your own thinking. This is a very tricky part of dealing with the disease. We who have the disease cannot always trust our own thinking. Our brain will tell us that it is the right thing to take that drink or smoke that joint or snort that line of cocaine. Our brain will lie to us. Instead of trusting our brain talking to us in our heads, we have to trust the principles we have decided to live by, the people whom we have learned will hold us accountable, and God.

Parents also must realize that their own brain does not always tell the truth. If you have been close to someone who has been in denial about the disease in the face of obvious evidence, you know what we mean. Most parents who have come into the program can look back and see that they had been in denial for a long time in the face of obvious indications of drug use. Even parents who can see this are vulnerable to falling back into denial and not seeing the evidence when faced with relapse. Therefore, we must stay open to what others are telling us.

Parents don't, and should not, blindly trust that whatever the counselor or their sponsor tells them is right. But parents should trust enough to really listen to the advice of the counselor—and if the advice does not sound right, they should talk to someone else and maybe several people, and should pray about it.

Ultimately, parents are responsible for their own decisions.

15. **Why do the parents have to work a program?**

They do not have to work a program, but it helps a great deal. The parents are dealing with a child who has a deadly disease. The disease presents some specific problems to the family, and the parents have to make decisions. There are cognitive and educational aspects to what the parents have to work through to decide what to do next as they support the young person through recovery. There also are emotional aspects. The parents have a myriad of feelings they must address before they can deal effectively with the disease. The feelings are about having a child in this kind of danger, the disease prejudice that exists in our culture, and what the parents may have done to contribute to their child's disease. Parents need a way to deal with these feelings on a day-to-day basis so that they do not get used by the disease in a way that gets in the way of recovery. Everybody has personality quirks, and the disease will use those quirks as fulcrums to get parents to do things that are not in the best interest of their child's recovery. For example, a parent who was herself raised by very controlling and rigid parents, may be over-committed to supporting her child's independence to the point of not being able to draw the line that says *we will not support you in our home while you are killing yourself with drug abuse.*

16. **Should I quit my job and monitor my child on a full-time basis?**

No. Your child is better off with an alternative peer group that will hold him accountable. When a child is using drugs or alcohol, no amount of parental supervision can prevent the use or turn the situation around. The parents can make a bigger impact by requiring their young person to work a program and stick with winners. There are other things you can do to have an important impact, but closely monitoring your young person is not one of them. On the other hand, you should stay aware. And if you notice behaviors that concern you, let the program counselor know.

17. **My son was at a program function at which the kids vandalized someone's property. Shouldn't the program functions at least be limited to activities that aren't against the law?**

We do not encourage or condone breaking the law in this program. But kids in the program do sometimes engage in criminal activities even after they begin to get sober. When it happens, we need to find out about it and deal with it by holding the kids who did it accountable. It's an opportunity to work with the kids on many fronts. What were they thinking? Did they stop and think? Looking back, what could they have done differently, and at what point? What are the effects of what they did? What can they do to make amends?

The kids will continue to be presented with situations in which they can practice skills they need to live responsibly. Until they learn those skills, they will react to some situations irresponsibly.

In the book *Beyond the Yellow Brick Road*, Bob Meehan discusses what he calls "fun felonies." He explains how much fun kids have breaking the law. He encourages parents to look back to when they were teenagers and the times they broke the law or rules. Those were some of our fondest memories—unless we got caught. His point is that it is part of being a teenager to enjoy breaking the rules and to not be mindful of the possible consequences. He does not suggest that there should be no consequences. Many readers remember this part of the book incorrectly. Meehan was explaining that this is normal behavior for a teenager; he was *not* suggesting that parents not concern themselves when their children commit mayhem. Suffering the consequences of their behavior is necessary for recovery and for becoming a responsible adult.

18. **We are divorced and my child's mother isn't supporting the program. She refuses to go to meetings and keeps alcohol in her home. I think the way that she relates to our daughter is contributing to her problem. I don't know what to do about it except take my ex to court, and I don't think my chances of winning would be good. What can I do?**

This is a difficult situation. You may be able to get an injunction from the courts so that the other parent cannot have access to the child. Or you may not be able to change the circumstances at all. But all is not lost. When we work with your daughter, we help her in getting and staying sober despite her circumstances. She may come to see that she needs to get out of her mother's environment, and will be able to achieve what you cannot in order to distance herself from that part of her family while she gets sober.

No parents can provide a safe environment outside the home. Nor can parents protect their children from being confronted by difficult situations. In the middle of trying to get sober, a child's grandparent will die, or the child will fail a grade at school, or his parents will get divorced. These experiences will hurt, and the addict may use them as an excuse to relapse in early recovery. But this is real-life stuff and it is in real life that the young person needs to have the skills to be able to stay sober. So while you may not be able to do anything about your ex-spouse contributing to the problem, pray about it and put some faith in your daughter's ability to make choices that support her sobriety.

Note that an experienced counselor can often help find ways to deal with this type of situation. Your experience or the group's experience may not be sufficient. This is one of the things the counselors are there for. Generally, the longer the counselor has been practicing, the more tricks she has in her bag.

19. **My daughter and her husband are addicts and I have been paying their rent and their car payments off and on for the past three years. I understand that I am enabling them by doing this, but they have my three grandchildren and I do it for them. It isn't fair for my grandchildren to suffer because of their parents. How can I protect my grandchildren and not enable my daughter?**

I agree with you that you should try to protect your grandchildren. But leaving them in the care of addicts is not protecting them. Your daughter has a disease that makes her too unwell to care for her children. What would you do if your daughter had a brain tumor that prevented her from hearing her baby crying, or from getting out of bed in the morning to make breakfast and get the children to school?

If your daughter and her husband can't manage their life so that they can pay their bills, you can bet that there are other bad things going on, as well. There are times when the parents are passed out and no one is taking care of their kids. There may be times when the parents have friends over who get loaded and go into the little girl's room or little boy's room and molest them. Your grandchildren are not being protected; they are being exposed to dangers they shouldn't be exposed to.

There is a way out and you may be the only person in your grandchildren's lives who will take a stand for them. You need to get the children out of that home. If you want to take on the day-to-day responsibility of parenting your grandchildren, you can ask for legal custody or go to court and fight for custody. If you don't choose to take on that responsibility, you can try to persuade your daughter and her husband to let the children go to a foster home, temporarily, while they get their lives and finances in order. If the parents are not willing, you can call your city or county's child protection agency and have the children placed in a safe home environment.

Again, consult a counselor for tactics and strategies.

20. **Who should be making the decisions about my child, the counselor or me?**

You, not the counselor. And it is important that you know you are making the decisions and that your child knows it. The counselor is your specialized adviser. You should listen to what he recommends. Counselors are trained and experienced in dealing with these issues. Also, they are not stopped by the codependent thinking to which all parents are vulnerable. But you make the decisions about the actions you will take.

Ideally, you and the counselor will agree on how to move forward. If you decide on a course of action different from what the counselor advises, the counselor, if possible, will support the approach you have chosen. He will support your decision for two reasons: first, because your approach might work, and might be a better approach for this particular young person; second, because a united approach is better than a divided approach, even if it is not the best approach.

Remember that the counselor is trained in young people's recovery. Parents are generally experienced in care-taking, nurturing and protecting. As much as the parents love and care about their child, your usual parenting style is probably not effective for dealing with the disease, and may even be counterproductive. Just as you would take the advice of medical doctors if your child had leukemia, you are advised to take the advice of recovery experts. The counselors know how best to handle most situations that parents face, but a counselor cannot administer what is needed without the parents' participation. Generally, parents need to give up their care-taking behaviors and support the counselors in requiring behaviors from their young person that are known to support recovery.

21. **Should I tell our family and friends that our child is in recovery?**

Generally speaking, you should handle this the way you would if your child had any other deadly disease. If she had leukemia, whom would you tell? Are you ready to step forward and treat this as a disease like leukemia? Any time you can say to your young person, yourself and anyone involved with your child, "This is a disease and you better treat it as a disease," the more effective you are going to be.

There may be some people it's best not to tell. If you have an old grandmother who is not going to be enabling your child and it would break her heart to learn of this, maybe you can spare the news. Or suppose you have an aunt who believes "if you would just . . . like she would . . .," this news could induce her to intervene in ways that will counteract what you are setting up to fight the disease. An estranged husband or wife who is an active user also would require a special approach. We recommend that you work with the counselor to develop a strategy for dealing with these special situations.

22. **Shouldn't we hospitalize our young person first?**

When sufficient hospital resources were available for treating sub-stance abuse, it was often helpful to go to a very controlled envi-ronment for a period of time to get recovery started. We could be sure of monitoring a solid 30 days of drying out, and we could get the user on a regimen that included hearing about the steps. A hos-pital usually wasn't necessary. Psychiatric nurses and psychiatrists weren't necessary. What was necessary was having good people working with the kids—people good at being with the addict for the first 30 days and at introducing them to the tools of sobriety.

We generally no longer have the resources available to start treat-ment in this way as fewer and fewer employer-provided health-care plans provide this benefit. Nor is it necessary. If the young person is willing to take part, even under duress, in activities that will lead to recovery on an outpatient basis, then why put him in a hospital? If he is not willing, or if he is incapable, then we find a more struc-tured situation such as an inpatient treatment center or hospital.

When they get out of the structured environment, it is essential that you hook them into a group of like-minded kids who value sobriety and learning the tools of recovery. They need the support of an alternative peer group and, often, a partially structured envi-ronment such as an intensive outpatient is a necessary "next step down."

Many parents want to put their young person in a hospital because it seems like it might provide a quick fix. Also, with the young per-son in a live-in situation, the parent doesn't have to deal with the child's day-to-day acting-out behaviors, and they get to feel com-fortable for awhile. Then, when their young person first comes back home, he's on his best behavior. For a short period of time, it seems like it worked. Then the child meets back up with his old friends and starts acting like a drug fiend again. Now the parents are stressed again and think they need to send their young person back to the hospital. But the truth is that their young person needs to learn how to stay sober here, in the real world. An inpatient program can help get recovery started, but the addict has to come back home—where the parents still have to do the work.

Again, inpatient treatment is usually not necessary. However, when a young person wants to get sober, but repeatedly fails, some time spent in an inpatient facility may help. But when he gets out, he will need to tie into an alternative peer group and learn how to stay sober outside of the controlled environment.

23. **How many meetings should I go to?**

As many as you can get to. Again, what if your child were diagnosed with leukemia and there were parent classes available to teach you how to support the treatment? How many classes would you attend? Also, you are going to need a long-term social structure to deal with this disease. The more meetings you attend, the quicker you are going to be able to set up that social structure. This will bring some relief to you and your child.

Our only caveat is that if you are going to so many meetings that you are starting to be resentful, then you need to do something different. For most people, two meetings each week, plus functions, is a good way to start.

24. **I'm not a "meeting kind" of person and I don't think I'll get anything out of listening to people talk about their problems.**

The meetings provide therapeutic benefits, information sharing and an opportunity for relationship-building. You get to hear what other people are doing to solve some of the problems that go with the disease. There is an opportunity for therapeutic sharing of your feelings and what is happening in your family. There is education about the disease and sharing about things that work. It is a forced activity that accelerates friendship building.

If you are not hearing solutions at meetings, then you aren't listening hard enough. You may be so caught up in the social side or the therapeutic side that you aren't hearing the solutions that other people are sharing. Try taking some notes. When members talk about something that worked, write it down. Being a "meeting type" of person has nothing to do with it. You are going to have to change if you want to change your young person's life. (See the previous question and answer.)

25. **I see the kids in the program smoking and using foul language and I wonder if I should let my child spend time with them.**

You might be in denial about what your young person already is involved in. Kids don't come to the program unless they were already involved, or feeling pressure to be involved, with an element of the culture that uses drugs and smokes and uses foul language. In fact, all American youth are heavily exposed to these behaviors, not only from peers, but from the media and pop culture. The difference is that once they enter the program, they aren't trying to fool you anymore about these things. Outside the program, they might stop smoking or cussing when the parents come around, to create an illusion that they aren't doing it. In the program, they might smoke and cuss in front of you, but they aren't doing drugs. And they don't do drugs when you are away. You need to get good at figuring out what is illusion and what is reality. The illusions just buy your young person another step toward the grave.

The kids do hold on to the smoking and cussing for awhile, and sometimes hold it in front of your face. They do it to this co-author. It's like their last in-your-face bravado. Their egos are involved. They don't want to get too "goody-goody" for you.

26. **We aren't religious and we understand that this is a spirituality-based program.**

The word "religious" implies taking part in a religion. This is not required for recovery. However, there are a few statistics about those who recover and those who do not. The number who recover from this disease, and do not reorient themselves toward some sort of lifestyle that embraces a purpose greater than what we can touch and feel on a daily basis, is almost zero. Of the ones who can give evidence to having reoriented themselves to a lifestyle that accepts a purpose or being beyond the carnal world, the success rate is almost 100 percent. If you are very logical or numbers-oriented, this is one of the strongest statistics we have, and you should pay attention to it.

How you develop this aspect that has been termed "spirituality" will be totally up to you. The term spirituality for many people has the connotation of religion. Spirituality often goes that way, but not necessarily. If the word spirituality puts you off, get rid of the word. Instead, embrace the concept of principles for living and of purpose for living. You have to move toward a purpose in living that goes beyond personal self-centeredness and I-want-what-I-want-when-I-want-it. How that develops is up to the individual.

27. **We are a religious family and are uncomfortable exposing our child to some vague spiritualism and vague higher-power concept.**

You may be religious, but your young person is *not*. For a person using drugs, chemicals are that person's god or purpose for living. The addict is using the chemicals to fulfill whatever position the family uses religious tenet to fulfill. For dealing with anxiety, the addict is turning to drugs. For dealing with frustration, he is turning to drugs.

The young person may be participating in religious activities out of habit or to throw the parents off, or both. The young person may be telling himself he is religious, but has replaced religion's purposes with a new faith of using drugs. That's not to discount that he may have been religious and spiritually oriented at one time. And a good counselor will be able to use this past practice of religion to help the addict return to the religion of his past. But be patient—this often takes more time than the parents or the counselor wish. Do not rush it; a common relapse pattern centers on abuse of religious organizations or practices.

28. **Should we move to another state or another part of town to get our kids away from drugs?**

You have started to learn about the disease and how insidious it is in our culture. If you are thinking about moving now, you may be under the illusion that there is a place to move to that won't have drugs in the culture or in the schools. There are no such places that we know of.

A young person with the disease will seek out the elements that support the disease wherever they are. You could move to an even worse situation. Or you could move to a better situation, but it may defocus your efforts to learn how to intervene with this disease, and make it easier for the young person to get around you and find the element that will support the disease.

The enemy is not the environment; the enemy is the disease and what is going on in your family. You need to focus on what you can do to support your young person in doing what he needs to do to get sober. Moving is a "quick fix" idea. If you move, your child will just isolate himself until he finds the element that feeds the disease.

There are, however, certain situations for which moving *may be* helpful. An example would be if you were living next door to lifelong friends with children who are using drugs. Other situations include if your child has serious gang involvement, or if you're living too close to a former spouse who uses. If you think you have a special situation, you should talk to the counselor about it.

If moving isn't necessary, it may be advisable to change schools in the beginning. Or you may need to let home-school your child for awhile. If school is one of the places where your child has been getting high, you can't expect him to stay sober there.

29. **We have a special event coming up (family vacation, high school graduation). Can we wait and deal with this after that event?**

Talk to the counselor. Consider how you would answer this if your child had another deadly disease. If she had leukemia, would you start the chemotherapy now or after graduation? You would talk to the doctor about the dangers of waiting. Maybe waiting a week or so would be OK. You will have to consider the acute ways of dying from the disease, which include overdosing, car accident, getting shot in the course of a crime contracting a sexually transmitted disease by having unprotected sex while under the influence of drugs.

If you put treatment off two weeks, there is some risk that it will be too late or the disease will have gotten worse during that time.

30. **My daughter is at college. Should I pull her out or wait until the end of the term?**

If she had a brain tumor, would you leave her at school? No, you would get the tumor under some control and make sure that your daughter knew how to treat the tumor while she was at college. Then you would let her return to school.

31. **What about our other kids?**

When there are other kids in the house, be aware that as you treat one of them you are treating them all. They all are watching to see how you handle the one who was caught.

In addition, special attention needs to be given to each of the siblings. The siblings of users either need to be in treatment themselves because they are using, or they need to be steered toward some preventive processes. The counselor can usually determine whether the sibling is using and whether she should be brought into the program. For siblings who have not used, you should find another group for them that has a high level of accountability. This might be a church group or a Scouting group. You will have to determine if there is accountability in the group by discussing it with the group leader. You will need to ask if the kids inform the leader if another member of the group is using.

If the leader responds that no one in the group uses, then there probably is no accountability.

32. **What about kids who have a dual diagnosis? Should they keep taking their medication?**

This decision has to be made with the child's physician. But parents should educate themselves on this subject and be informed decision-makers.

Before we begin discussing dual diagnosis, we should have some sort of understanding of the term. Historically, the term was introduced to describe a situation in which the person diagnosed with a substance abuse-related disorder was concurrently suffering from another psychological disorder. Although suffering from any psychological disorder officially qualified a patient for dual diagnosis, initially the term was usually used to describe those suffering from attending disorders characterized by severe delusions, hallucinations and phobias. These attending disorders usually were those that could only be effectively controlled with regular medication regimens.

In the past several years, this definition has evolved practically to include people suffering from chemical-use disorders and other psychological disorders characterized by mood and thought patterns considered problematic. Unlike the disorders (characterized by delusions, hallucinations and phobias) present in the original definition, there still is great controversy surrounding the treatment of the attending mood and though-pattern disorders present in the new and wider definition of dual diagnosis. Huge controversy rages around the use and effectiveness of medications and talk therapies.

Most kids who come into the program have been diagnosed as having some psychological disorder. In most cases, the diagnosis was made after the young person started using illegal chemicals, but before the parents or the psychologist or psychiatrist had knowledge of it.

Treating someone with dual diagnosis is very tricky. Here is a common scenario:

A young person's school grades drop when he starts smoking pot and taking acid. The parents take him to a psychiatrist, who diagnoses the child with Attention Deficit Disorder (ADD). The psychiatrist starts him on Ritalin. Ritalin (snorted, not swallowed) becomes another drug the child abuses as a means of getting high. Does the young person really have ADD? Or did the substance abuse cause the symptoms of ADD? It's impossible to tell until after the kid gets some sobriety.

Other common diagnoses the kids come labeled with include Manic Depressive Disorder, Obsessive Compulsive Disorder and clinical depression. The question then is whether this underlying psychological disorder contributed to the person's decision to use chemicals (self-medication, perhaps), or if the effect of substance abuse on the person's behavior and on brain chemistry produced false evidence for the presence of a psychological disorder.

The parents are left to struggle with whether to take their child off the medication. A complicating factor is that while the chemical-dependency counselors have a working knowledge of psychological disorders and may have a profound knowledge of your child and his history of chemical use, they are not licensed to, or have the expertise to, diagnose psychological disorders or recommend treatment for those disorders. At the same time, the psychologists and psychiatrists who are diagnosing kids with these disorders generally have little knowledge of substance abuse and the treatment of chemical dependence. Furthermore, they tend to ignore the possibility of the presence of substance abuse and its effects.

In 1998, University of St. Thomas (Houston, Texas) psychology professors Anette Edens and Nicole Chaloupka conducted a study to determine the extent of the problem of improper diagnosis and treatment of adolescents using alcohol or illegal drugs. Through informal interviews with 25 program parents, they found that the "adolescents participated in a total of 96 failed treatment attempts, averaging 24 months of failed treatment apiece, before entering rehabilitation treatment for substance abuse." They summarized the result of their study as follows:

"... *adolescents participate in an average of four separate treatments prior to entering treatment for chemical dependency. Half of the prior treatments involved individual therapy for the adolescent, and the most frequent providers (32 percent) were psychiatrists. Very few (19 percent) of the prior treatments consider alcohol or drug use to be a primary concern. In fact, 64 percent of the prior providers either are unaware that the adolescent is using drugs or alcohol or chose not to divulge this information to the parent. Sixty percent of adolescent sub-*

stance abusers are being prescribed from one to seven different simultaneous medications to treat diagnoses including major depression, attention deficit disorder, oppositional defiant disorder, bipolar disorder, anxiety disorder, personality disorder N.O.S., and Tourette's Syndrome. At the time of data collection 23 percent were continuing to take medication for depression and/or attention deficit disorder, but all symptoms in the other adolescents had remitted upon sustained sobriety.

"Parents reporting psychiatric therapy to be harmful cite their children's abuses of the medications prescribed, the time wasted in treatment, and the costs involved. Parents reporting prior treatments to be helpful feel that the therapy is not helpful to the child directly, but at least provides the parent a resource with whom they can share their concerns about their child."

Adolescents using drugs generally do not tell their parents or therapists. Before diagnosing young people with psychological disorders, health-care professionals need to determine if substance abuse is present. While it is not foolproof, this can be done using a sample of hair and a surprise urinalysis. These bodily samples, when tested, will reveal the commonly used illegal drugs. It will not pick up the use of alcohol.

Discuss your child's substance-abuse issues with the physician prescribing medication for your child. Together, you may decide to take the child off medication and see if the symptoms indicating psychiatric disorder go away with sobriety.

33. **My child is totally unwilling. He doesn't even think he has a problem. Doesn't a person have to want help in order to change?**

The idea that "nobody will change unless he wants to change" is a commonly accepted notion that can lead parents away from recovery. Don't get hooked by this. Nobody walks in the door because he wants to stop getting high. He wants out of the troubles that getting high has created for him. He wants to get out from under trouble with the law, work, school, parents, other relationships or his health. It is when these results of using drugs or alcohol become unbearable that someone is usually ready to get sober. This is commonly referred to as "hitting bottom."

Early recovery means accelerating the time the sufferer wants to get sober, and supporting him in doing so. This acceleration can come from being attracted into the program and the recovery activities first by the other kids and the social functions, and then by the promises offered by recovery and the individual's own progress toward a healthy lifestyle.

Other times the desire to get sober is accelerated when the parents cease to protect their young person by protecting him from the consequences of the disease and no longer enabling him to use drugs. This may include not bailing him out of jail if he is arrested (at least not immediately), not running interference for him at school, or not giving him money. It may also mean no longer allowing him to live in the family home unless he is willing to work a program of recovery. This is often referred to as "raising their bottom." The idea is to let the addict suffer the consequences of using so that he will become uncomfortable enough to want to get sober. The earlier this occurs in the course of the disease, the less damage there will be to the sufferer's life. The addict may not have to lose his job or family or life before he is ready to get sober.

References

Branden, Nathaniel, *The Power of Self-Esteem*, 67–68, Deerfield Beach, Florida: Health Communications, Inc.1992.

Beattie, Melody, *Codependent No More: How to Stop Controlling Others and Start Caring for Yourself*, San Francisco, California: A Harper/Hazelden Book, Harper & Row, 1987. Paraphrased from Chapter 4.

The names and circumstances in personal accounts included in this book have been fictionalized to protect the privacy of the subjects and their families.

About the Authors

Recovering from years of personal addiction, National Association of Addiction and Drug Abuse Counselors's 2001 National Counselor of the Year, John C. Cates, has counseled, designed programs, and spoken worldwide about chemical dependency for more 27 years. Living in Houston with his family, he holds a master's degree in counseling, manages a private practice and directs Lifeway.

Jennifer Cummings, mother of two thriving adults, spent five years studying and doing all she could to save her children from addiction and self-destructive behavior. She was supported by the work of Lifeway and Palmer Drug Abuse Program, Alternative Peer Group programs, and Covenant House in Houston. She serves on the Cornerstone advisory board.